Greensboro Century

The Gate City
1900-1999

STEPHEN H. PROVOST

Century Cities Publishing 2022
A division of Dragon Crown Books
Martinsville, Virginia   ✦   Fresno, California
San Luis Obispo, California
All rights reserved

ISBN-13: 978-1-949971-28-6

Century Cities

Century Cities Publishing was created to celebrate and preserve the history of midsized and smaller American cities during the 20th century. Narratives are presented in timeline form, drawing on major milestones and lesser-known stories from 1900 to 1999. From athletic champions to retail milestones, from city leaders to entertainers, these books provide a panoramic overview of vibrant, growing cities as they came into their own.

Books in this series

Cambria Century, 2021

Charleston Century, 2021

Danville Century, 2021

Fresno Century, 2021

Goldfield Century, 2021

Greensboro Century, 2022

Huntington Century, 2021

Roanoke Century, 2021

San Luis Obispo Century, 2021

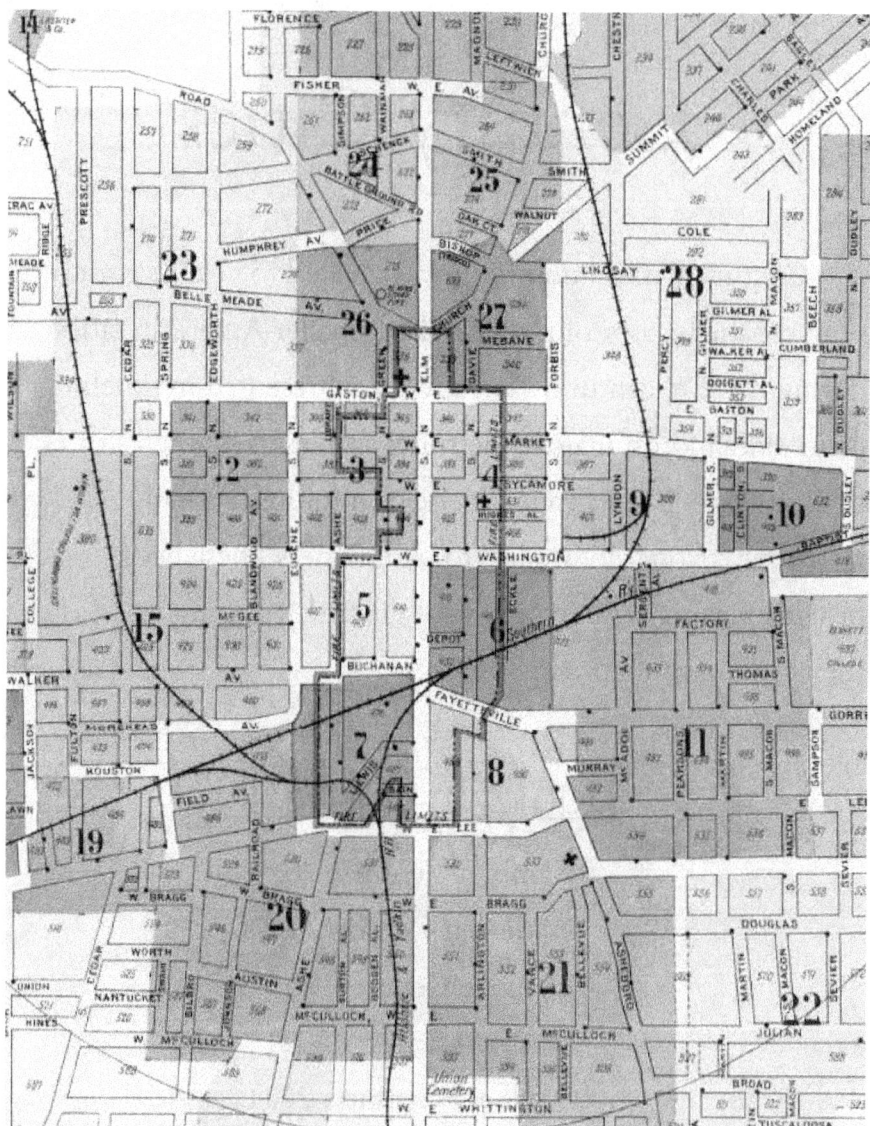
Sanborn Fire Insurance map of downtown Greensboro area in 1919.
Library of Congress

GREENSBORO CENTURY

Contents

"Towns change; they grow or diminish, but hometowns remain as we left them."

Jayne Anne Phillips,
Novelist

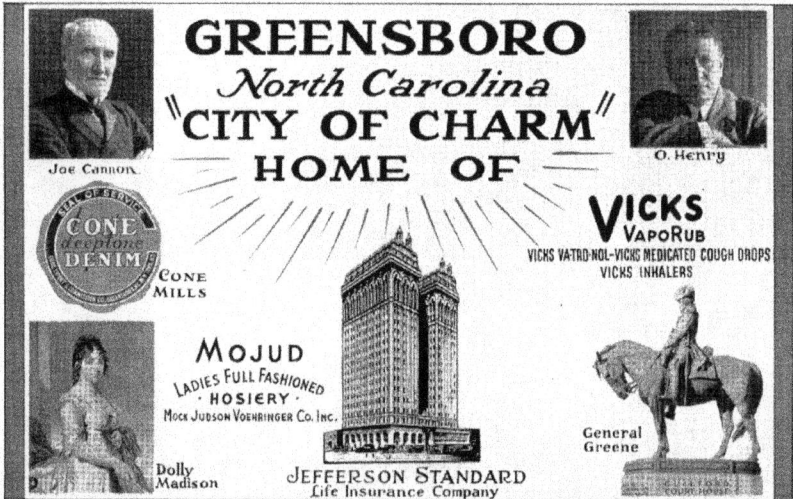

This vintage postcard spotlights significant Greensboro landmarks, industries, and residents from the 1915-1930 period. *University of North Carolina Libraries*

The Greensboro Grand Opera House, which also housed City Hall, is seen in this picture c. 1908. *University of North Carolina Libraries*

The Southern Railway Station, completed in June of 1899 on South Elm Street, was emblematic of Greensboro's status as the Gate City. It's seen here sometime between 1905 and 1915. *University of North Carolina Libraries*

Introduction

Greensboro was a natural fit for my *Century Cities* series. Like two cities I've profiled previously — Roanoke and Danville — it's within an hour's drive of Martinsville, Virginia, where I wrote this book.

Greensboro is a beautiful city filled with history, charm, and character. There are plenty of trees in Greensboro, but it's not named for the area's verdant vegetation. It's named after Nathanael Greene, a major general in the Revolutionary War. (The last "e" was dropped, although it's retained on Greene Street downtown.)

Today, it's the third-largest city in North Carolina, behind Charlotte and Raleigh, having recently surpassed 300,000 residents. That makes it the second-largest city I've profiled to date, behind Fresno, California.

And it's also the largest, and easternmost, in the Piedmont Triad region that also includes High Point just to the southwest and Winston-Salem farther west. It was perfectly situated to become a transportation hub for the region, with 60 trains a day passing through in 1891, when it earned its nickname, the Gate City.

Not as many trains pass through now, but the nickname has stuck. There's even a Gate City Boulevard that runs through town.

The 20th century saw Greensboro grow from a city of barely 10,000 people at its outset to a bustling metropolis of more than 220,000 by the end of the millennium. In the meantime, it gave birth to a textile boom, was the site of historic civil rights protests, hosted a major golf tournament and even had its own pro basketball team.

The famed short story writer O. Henry worked at a downtown pharmacy before the turn of the century, and the new millennium has seen the construction of a modern baseball stadium (First Horizon Stadium) and the Steven Tanger Performing Arts Center.

Plenty of stories can be told of the city from the 19th and 21st centuries. *Greensboro Century* tells the story of what happened in between.

Textile Town

1900–1909

The County Courthouse and Post Office as it appeared in the early 20th century. *University of North Carolina Libraries*

1900

Community

The City Hall and Grand Opera House opened at the northeast corner of Friendly and Elm. ...

The Bessemer Truck Farm opened around this time, marking the first commercial development in the Bessemer area. Subdivisions would come later, starting with Bessemer Highland in 1918 and Bessemer Heights in 1923. Bessemer Park and South Bessemer appeared in 1927.

The community would house a mix of white-collar and

blue-collar workers, including mill employees. ...

Pomona Mill Village housed 1,000 people by this time: workers at the Pomona Cotton Mill and Pomona Terra Cotta Company.

Milestones

Greensboro enjoyed a significant jump in growth, from just 3,317 the year before to 10,035 at the turn of the new century — an increase of 202.5 percent.

1901

Business

Greensboro Loan and Trust opened the doors to its new building July 25, with the *Greensboro Telegram* declaring it "one of the handsomest of its kind in the State."

The building at 319 South Elm showcased the Italian Renaissance style that was popular in that day. Banking offices and a vault with 102 safe deposit boxes were on the first floor, with other offices on the second floor and apartments on the third.

The vault itself was extremely secure. It was opened by a time lock and then a combination, then by turning a wheel, and the door was too heavy to be opened or shut by a single person.

Greensboro Loan and Trust's new building went up within a year or two after another financial institution, Southern Loan and Trust, constructed a five-story building at 110 East Market Street. From the top of that building, the *Telegram* reported, you could take in a panoramic view of Greensboro in three directions (the fourth was blocked by trees), and could even catch glimpses of the Blue Ridge Mountains in the distance.

The building had a restaurant on the fourth floor alongside apartments, with more apartments on the top floor. The structure housed the loan company and its affiliate, Pilot Life Insurance, until the company moved to Sedgefield in 1928. Ten years later, the building was destroyed.

The West Market Church, foreground, was formally dedicated in 1901. *Author photo*

Faith

The sanctuary of the aptly named West Market Church was dedicated. It had been completed eight years earlier, but dedication was put off until the debt on the building had been paid.

The congregation itself dated back to the 1820s, 12 years before Greensboro itself was founded. A predecessor to the new sanctuary at 302 West Market Street, a small two-story building, had been constructed in 1831. It was the first church building in the area.

Government

William H. Osborne was elected mayor. He served until 1903.

1902

Baseball

Greensboro made its minor-league baseball debut, joining the Class-D North Carolina League alongside the Charlotte Hornets, Durham Bulls, New Bern Truckers, Raleigh Red Birds, and Wilmington Sailors.

The Greensboro Farmers, managed by Jim Kelly, played their games in 2,000-seat Cone Park at Bessemer and Summit avenues, a major intersection later occupied by strip malls like the Summit and Northeast shopping centers. (The ballpark was developed by the Cone Mills textile plant, and company teams also played there.)

The Charlotte Hornets won the pennant with a 44-12 record, while the Farmers finished in fourth place at 33-30 in Kelly's first season as a manager. The Farmers — and the league as a whole — folded after just one season, but Kelly went on to manage five other teams in the Carolinas and Virginia through the 1920 season, compiling a career record of 404 wins and 342 losses.

Community

The Southern Land and Trust Company laid out the Edgeville neighborhood, between the mills of northeast Greensboro and Bessemer, which was separate from the city at that point.

Edgeville was largely a working-class neighborhood, home
to mill workers, and didn't really start growing until the 1920s
It was annexed to Greensboro by 1935.

A Greensboro streetcar offers a ride to the ballgame. *University of North Carolina Libraries*

Recreation

Electric streetcar companies began operating in cities
across the country just after the turn of the century. Many of
those lines connected downtowns with new suburbs or areas
targeted for development.

To maximize ticket sales, these companies often created
destinations at the end of the line — things like parks,
bandstands, and amusement areas with rides and other
attractions — or built lines to destinations that already existed.

Greensboro was no exception.

In this case, the Greensboro Electric System linked
Greensboro to Pomona, with the line terminating at Spring
Garden Street. That's where Lindley Park was built. The 22-acre
site on a hilltop along Masonic Drive was named for J. Van

Lindley, who donated the land to the company on one condition: that it be used as park space for 15 years.

"The street car service to the park at Pomona was inaugurated yesterday," the *Greensboro Patriot* reported on June 25. "The buildings at the park will soon be completed, and it will be one of the most attractive spots in the county."

The first buildings to go up were a vaudeville stage and a dance pavilion that stayed open until 1 in the morning. Other attractions soon joined them, including bowling alleys, soda fountains, a refreshment stand, a summer theater with 1,000 seats, and a lake.

Another Greensboro trolley, seen in the 1910s. *University of North Carolina Libraries*

Predictably, the presence of the park and trolley line created demand for residential lots in the area. On June 1, 1904, an auction was held for lots along the line between the city limits and Lindley Park. According to the *Greensboro Patriot*, the auction attracted a large number of people, with 59 lots being sold.

One buyer, E.M. Moore, purchased a lot for $385, which might not sound like much until you realize that would add up to something like $11,000 in 2022.

The park continued to operate until 1917, when the 15-year conditional use expired and the land was sold to a developer with plans for a residential subdivision.

The J.W. Scott & Company building, where the wholesale grocer operated for nearly seven decades starting in 1902. *Author photo*

Retail

J.W. Scott & Co. set up shop with a dry goods and notions store at 113 West Washington Street in the fall. The three-story building was erected on the site of Cyrus Mendenhall's home, "The Elms," which was moved up the street. The store's motto: "The best seeds money will buy. (No trash sold)."

Founder John W. Scott, a Civil War veteran, had returned home penniless after being captured and thrown in a Delaware prison. After two years of farming, he went to work as a sales clerk and founded his own retail grocery business in 1871. Dry goods and notions were added to his stock seven years after that.

Scott was still running the place in 1914, when the *Greensboro Patriot* declared: "The 70 years of John W. Scott, of Greensboro, rest lightly upon him, for he feels as young as any boy of the city. The young friend he calls 'old man,' and the old crony 'young man' ...

"Young himself, in spite of experiences calculated to age him, he is interested in everything the city is interested in, active in business, church and municipal affairs, and withal modest, pleasant and very companionable."

The business Scott founded operated as wholesale grocer on West Washington Street until 1970, and the building was converted for use as office space around 1990.

1903

Government

T.J. Murphy began a two-year term as mayor. He would later serve three more terms, from 1911 to 1917.

1904

Business

Charles C. Hudson founded the Hudson Overall Company over the Coe Brothers Grocery store on South Elm Street.

Hudson had been working in a Greensboro overall factory for 25 cents a day. But when that business closed, he found himself at loose ends, so to speak. So he and his brother

Homer purchased several of the sewing machines and started their own company.

The company, later renamed Blue Bell, would become the largest maker of exclusively wholesale overalls. It returned sales of $156,000 in 1918, and a year later moved to a new factory at 626 South Elm.

The Blue Bell Jeans factory built in 1918 still stands, now used as the Old Greensboro Gateway Center. *Author photo*

In 1926, it would be purchased by a Kentucky-based company called Big Ben Manufacturing, but its headquarters would stay in Greensboro. The biggest change, however, came in 1943 when the company bought the Casey Jones Company — and with it the rights to an obscure brand name.

It would become a household name in years to come: Wrangler. ...

The new McAdoo Building at 113 South Elm had a distinctive look for one important reason: It was narrow. Very narrow. In fact, the new five-story building almost looked top-heavy because it was just a little over 26 feet wide.

The $30,000 building was completed in six months' time.

It initially housed the Greensboro Life Insurance Company on the first floor, with physicians and cotton brokers' offices above and the Greensboro Elks Lodge on the top floor.

But the building's height and narrow footprint may have posed structural problems, because the top two floors were removed in the 1930s.

Fire

The *Greensboro Patriot* described it as "Greensboro's greatest fire" and "one of the most thrilling catastrophes ever witnessed in the South" when the main dormitory of the State Normal and Industrial College burned to the ground.

More than 300 women, many of whom were asleep at the time, were roused and had to flee the conflagration one evening in early January. Many left their clothes behind to burn, but all escaped safely, even as the flames spread to two smaller brick buildings: a laundry and a heating plant. Both were destroyed.

The fires started in a kitchen at the rear of the west hall, an extension that had been built onto the main dormitory.

St. Leo's Hospital, seen in 1907. *University of North Carolina Libraries*

Health Care

The Sisters of Charity opened St. Leo's Hospital on Summit Avenue. It would operate until 1953, when it was converted into Notre Dame Catholic High School. The school remained open until 1968 and was torn down two years later.

1905

Baseball

Baseball returned to Greensboro after a two-year absence — but not for long. The new Virginia-Carolina League, a Class-D outfit like its predecessor, only lasted through August 19 before disbanding.

Greensboro was in the cellar of the four-team league when it ceased operations, only managing a 36-47 record to bring up the rear behind the Danville Tobacconists, Charlotte Hornets and a team that played in Salisbury and Spencer before moving to Winston-Salem on July 17.

Farmers pitcher Buck Hooker had played three games with the Cincinnati Reds in 1902 and 1903.

South Elm Street c. 1907. University of North Carolina Libraries

Business

Another tall building went up on Elm Street, which was quickly becoming a corridor of what, at the time, qualified as skyscrapers.

The latest was the five-story City National Bank Building at 125 South Elm, which became the tallest building in the city on completion in July. But it wasn't known by that name for long. Dixie Fire Insurance moved in shortly after it opened, and the building became known as the Dixie Building.

The McAdoo Hotel on Elm Street as it appeared in the early 20th century. *University of North Carolina Libraries*

Community

William McAdoo laid out the plan for McAdoo Heights, providing homes for many workers in the Revolution and White Oak mills. It included a small commercial district consisting of two-story brick buildings on State Street.

McAdoo was the son of Calvin Hicks McAdoo, who'd built the McAdoo Hotel on Elm Street back in 1870 ...

The American Suburban Corporation laid out Piedmont Heights, a neighborhood populated largely by lumber workers and employees of industrial sites along Lee Street and the Southern Railroad corridor.

Education

Immanuel College, founded two years earlier in Concord, moved to a 13-acre campus in Greensboro at Luther and East Market streets. A segregated school for Black students, it operated on three levels: as a seminary, a junior college, and a residential high school.

The school closed in 1961. Among its noted alumni was actor Gregg Morris, who appeared from 1966 to 1973 as Barney Collier on television's *Mission: Impossible*.

The Greensboro Fire Department Hose Company No. 4 Southside station was built in 1905. *Author photo*

Fire

Construction was complete on the G.F.D. Hose Company No. 4 Southside, a two-story first station on what is today Martin Luther King Jr. Drive (then known as Asheboro Street).

Government

L.J. Brandt was elected mayor, serving until 1907.

The building that once housed the historic Porter's Drug Store is seen for lease on Elm Street in 2022. *Author photo*

Health

Lunsford Richardson, a pharmacist, started a company based on some medicinal remedies he'd developed.

After studying at Davidson College, he moved to Selma,

southeast of Raleigh, to work for his brother-in-law in his medical practice. Richardson's job there was to dispense pharmaceuticals, and he took the opportunity to experiment with different formulas.

He moved to Greensboro in 1890, where he purchased a downtown drugstore that had once employed William Sydney Porter — the famous short-story author, O. Henry (Porter's Drug at 121 South Elm Street). According to legend, Richardson's three-syllable name wouldn't fit neatly on the containers for his salves, ointments, pills, and tonics, so he used his brother-in-law's much shorter name instead.

His remedies included things like Turtle Oil Liniment, Chill Tonic, Yellow Pine Tar Cough Syrup, and Tar Heel Sarsaparilla. The most successful formula, however, was one he developed for his son back in the late 1800s. Just a baby at the time, the boy had something called croup: coughing and chest congestion. To treat the condition, Richardson developed a menthol- and eucalyptus-based salve he called Magic Croup Salve.

Six years after Richardson founded his company, his son — by then a salesman for the company — suggested that his father stop selling the other products in his line to focus on the Magic Croup Salve. But he didn't care for the name. It called for something more distinctive, he thought, and so he suggested a change. Retaining the name of Richardson's former boss, the pharmacist, he proposed something punchier and alliterative. So it came to pass that Vicks VapoRub was born, named for old Dr. Joshua Vick in Selma.

The plan to focus on VapoRub, which was rubbed on the chest so that its potent vapors could help clear congestion, worked like a charm. Coupons were printed in newspapers, and free samples were deposited in mailboxes. Sales of Vicks soared during the Spanish flu epidemic of 1918-19, reaching $2.9 million in a single year.

Richardson died of pneumonia in 1919, and his sons carried the company forward. Production was automated, and Vicks was listed on the New York Stock Exchange in 1925. Company sales reached $1 billion in 1979, and Vicks was sold to Dow Chemical four years later, eventually becoming part of Procter & Gamble.

Officers of Proximity Manufacturing Company and White Oak Cotton are seen in 1909, with Ceasar Cone at the center of the

Industry

Brothers Moses and Ceasar Cone got their start as grocery salesmen from Baltimore, but they didn't make their fortune selling lettuce.

They wove an empire in textiles, opening a 200-loom denim factory called Proximity Mill at Greensboro in 1896, and building another denim plant called the White Oak Cotton Mill in 1905 at a cost of $1.25 million. (The Proximity Mill was named for its location near cotton fields, rail lines, and warehouses.)

Early postcards show overviews of the Proximity Textile Mill, top, and the White Oak Mill, above.

The Cones were nothing if not ambitious: "Ceasar and I are to build another Denim Mill" which would have "1,000 looms, the idea being to give us a denim business of say $2,500,000 –

and to Control that business in the U.S," Moses said in 1902 of his plans for White Oak.

By 1907, two years after it opened, that mill had 1,000 employees and not 1,000 but 2,000 looms with 60,000 spindles. And a year later, the company was the top denim producer in the world.

Each of the Cones' mills was at the heart of a company-owned village that included everything from schools to recreation centers, shops, and churches. Altogether, the mill villages had living quarters for nearly 2,700 workers and covered some 450 acres at their peak.

They were eventually sold off in the 1940s.

The Cone name lived on in Greensboro. It's on the Moses Cone Memorial Hospital, which opened in 1953 on North Elm Street; Cone Elementary School at 2501 North Church Street; Cone Boulevard; and the Cone Ballroom at UNC-Greensboro, reflecting the family's civic involvement and donations.

Another early postcard shows the White Oak Mill, with worker housing in the foreground.

White Oak Cotton Mills housing up close, as seen in 1912. *Lewis Hine Wickes, Library of Congress*

Journalism

Carl Duncan founded the *Daily Industrial News* as a Republican newspaper.

1906

Community

The Greensboro Carnegie Library opened at Gaston Street and Library Place.

Fast Food

People began saying "Yum Yum" for the first time when Yum Caesar Better Ice Cream and hot dogs opened in Greensboro.

At first, W.B. Aydelette didn't have a full-fledged shop; he started off selling peanuts and other snacks from a pushcart.

Then came the ice cream.

The flavor that made his business stand out? Pink ice cream mixed with Grape Nuts cereal. Other flavors were added over the years, such as eggnog, coconut, and chocolate raspberry. Cones were made using an old waffle iron, and hot dogs found a place on the menu before World War II for those who weren't in the mood for cold and creamy treats.

It was out of necessity: Aydelette couldn't find enough sugar to make his ice cream.

Yum Yum Better Ice Cream was still in business as of 2022, although at a different location than the original site where it was founded in 1906. *Author photos*

But the hot dogs, served with chili, mustard, onions, and coleslaw, were such a hit that they outsold the ice cream — and it wasn't even close: He might sell 300 cones and 2,500 dogs on a hot summer day.

Aydelette and his wife Lenora put $1,000 down on the $8,775 purchase price for a parcel of land at Forest and Spring Garden streets in 1921. It was a strategic location near the North Carolina College for Women (later University of North Carolina at Greensboro).

The college grew and eventually began admitting men in 1963, and while that growth meant new business, it wasn't necessarily all good for Yum Yum. In 1972, the state seized the land where Yum Yum stood for expansion: It needed the site for an administrative building.

Yum Yum reopened up the road at 1219 Spring Garden Street.

"The new location wasn't going to be near as good as this one has been, though," Aydelette said. "It was a sad day when they told us that we were going to have to move."

But at least Aydelette got something out of it: $183,595 to be exact, the amount the state paid him for his property.

Recreation

W.F. Clegg planned a number of new amusements at Lindley Park as it prepared to open for the season in April. Among them was a moving picture machine that would present scenes from a recent prize fight and showing the New York Fire Department rescuing people from the top story of a tenement.

A casino was also planned, with vaudeville and comic opera performances nightly during the summer.

1908

Baseball

The Greensboro Champs were charter members of the Carolina Association and lived up to their name as the league's first champions. The Champs finished the season at 51-38, 2½ games ahead of the second-place Greenville Spinners, the only other team with a winning record in the six-team league.

Walter Hammersley was the ace of the staff, compiling a 22-8 record, as no one in the lineup hit above .250.

Journalism

The *Daily Industrial News* went belly-up, and what was left of it was purchased by two newsmen from Asheville, Walter Hildebrand — whose Republican leanings were in line with its the viewpoint of the old newspaper — and George Crater. It was soon renamed the *Greensboro Daily News*.

Milestones

Egbert Roscoe Murrow, better known to radio listeners and TV viewers as Edward R. Murrow, was born April 25 south of Greensboro at Polecat Creek. Egbert was a royal name, once worn in the eighth century by the King of Wessex. But Edward sounded better in the 20th, so Edward it was.

Murrow became famous for his radio reporting from London during the Blitz in World War II and had a radio program called *Hear It Now* that evolved into a TV show that launched in 1951 called *See It Now*.

The show is best remembered for Murrow's focus on McCarthyism: Senator Joseph McCarthy's pursuit of alleged communist sympathizers (known as the Red Scare) that

Edward R. Murrow, a native of the Greensboro area and a future acclaimed broadcast journalist, is seen here in 1953.

resulted in some artists, entertainers, and others being blacklisted.

Murrow commented:

"Nations have lost their freedom while preparing to defend it, and if we in this country confuse dissent with disloyalty, we deny the right to be wrong."

Murrow, a chain-smoker, would die of lung cancer in 1965 at the age of 57.

Prohibition

North Carolina became the first state to adopt a prohibition on alcohol May 26, by a decisive vote of 62 percent to 38 percent.

The margin was even bigger in Greensboro, where residents voted nearly 3-1 to go dry: The tally was 1,159 votes in favor of prohibition, with just 392 opposed.

1909

The Cascade Saloon on Elm Street was among the businesses affected when North Carolina became the first state to adopt a prohibition on the sale of alcohol. *Author photo*

Baseball

The Champs, renamed the Patriots in 1909, nonetheless repeated as champs of the Carolina Association with a 65-44 record in their second and final season under manager James McKevitt.

Tony Walters, who toiled for eight seasons in the minors,

won a career-high 25 games against 12 losses to lead the pitching staff. Outfielder Jack Anthony led the team at the plate with a .269 average and 20 doubles.

The team would revert to the Champs name for the 1910 season, but this time, it didn't work out as well for them: They finished last in the six-team league. Adopting the Patriots moniker again in 1911, they finished second behind Winston-Salem with a record of 66-43.

The team would continue to operate through 1917, with the league switching its name to the North Carolina State League in 1913, but never again finished above .500.

Cinema

The Southern Amusement Company opened the 610-seat Bijou Theatre at 219 Elm Street. It was closed by 1932.

Golf

A.W. McAlister, president of Pilot Life Insurance, saw a game of golf being played, and he was intrigued. So he bought some clubs and brought them back to Greensboro.

McAlister then laid out a five-hole pitch-and-putt golf course that was open to anyone who wanted to play — free of charge. Golfers just walked up, hung their jackets on the branches of an oak tree, and teed off. From those humble beginnings sprang the Greensboro Country Club.

Government

E.J. Stafford was elected Greensboro's mayor for two years.

Six years later, he would be elected for two more terms.

Retail

The Great Atlantic & Pacific Tea Company, popularly known as A&P, entered the Greensboro market with a new store at 326 South Elm Street.

The Bijou opened on Elm Street in 1909 and remained open for about two decades. *elmorovivo, Creative Commons 2.0, cinematreasures*

Chasing the Sky

1910–1919

1910

Industry

Herman and Emanuel Sternberger had been managing a store in Clio, South Carolina, when they moved to Greensboro and founded the Revolution Cotton Mill.

Having been persuaded to make the move by Moses Cone, the Sternbergers quickly followed in his footsteps by establishing a highly successful mill along with a self-contained community for the workers. The mill village included schools, stores, and a YMCA, and essential services such as a physician, dentists, and nurses.

The Sternbergers also built houses and charged workers $4 a room in rent.

Milestones

Greensboro's population was 15,895, an increase of 58.4 percent in just 10 years.

1911

Golf

The Greensboro Country Club mailed prospectuses to "professional and business men of the city," around the first of the year, informing them of the club's formal incorporation.

In addition to golf, the new club planned to offer recreational pastimes such as tennis, croquet, and bowling.

The club was offering two kinds of membership. Locals could pay $100 (about $3,000 in 2022 dollars) to the development company that was buying the land or $100 for club membership, which covered the first 10 months, and $2 a month thereafter.

Things moved quickly from there. By March 31, the club had purchased a 50-acre tract of land a mile and a half from the courthouse and arranged for a trolley line to be built to it.

The Greensboro Country Club in 2022.
Author photo

A new 250-foot-long clubhouse was built with porches overlooking the club's land. The basement housed bowling lanes, game rooms, locker rooms, and a kitchen; the main floor consisted of a living room with a huge fireplace, a reading room, and a dining room that could seat as many as 60 people. Cloak rooms and baths were on the top floor.

The $500 clubhouse went up near the oak tree where golfers had hung their coats to play on A.W. McAlister's five-hole pitch-and-putt course a couple of years earlier. McAlister served as president of the club, as he would for the Sedgefield Country Club when it was founded 15 years later.

McAlister was so enamored of the game that he even published a book titled *The Eternal Verities of Golf: A Study in Philosophy and the Ancient Game* in 1911. But he was a businessman, too, and the new country club served as a drawing card for development in the area.

The result was an upscale neighborhood called Irving Park.

The Dixie Building added another story to stay even with the new Banner Building as the tallest in the city. *Author photo*

1912

Business

The Banner Building opened in October at 119 North Elm, giving Greensboro its first six-story building. It was equipped with elevators and telephone lines to 82 offices.

But the owners of the seven-year-old Dixie Building didn't like the fact that they'd been topped as the city's tallest building, so they added another story of their own. Greensboro now had two six-story buildings on Elm Street.

They remained the tallest buildings in town until plans were announced in 1918 for a nine-story structure at 100-102 Elm Street to house the American Exchange National Bank.

Industry

The Cone brothers built a cloth-printing plant called Proximity Print Works, one of the earliest facilities of its kind in the southern United States. ...

The Daily Bread Flour mill at 816 South Elm. *Author photo*

North State Milling was founded to manufacture Daily Bread Flour and Joy Brand Corn Meal, along with bran, livestock feed, and hen scratch. The plant at 816 South Elm Street originally contained wooden silos inside; the imposing metal silos on the outside were added later.

1913

Community

Greensboro covered two square miles, had five banks, a public library with 10,000 volumes. Sixty-one industries employed 1,132 people. It was served by St. Leo's hospital, "one of the great hospitals of the South," along with five other private hospitals and sanitariums. So said the city directory.

1914

Industry

The Cones Brothers' Proximity company began producing denim for Levi's jeans.

Weather

Greensboro had a hot time on July 27 — the hottest time ever, in fact, as the mercury reached a record 104 degrees.

1915

Education

The A. and M. College for the Colored Race changed its name to the Negro Agricultural and Technical College of North Carolina.

Retail

The Gilmer Bros. Company announced it was opening its Greensboro Sample Store at 316 South Elm Street, opposite Odell Hardware. The new store, which was to open September 11, boasted it would be have approximately $20,000 worth of mill samples for sale at 60 cents on the dollar.

The Gilmer line of products included dry goods, notions, blankets, quilts, towels, pillowcases, underwear, hosiery, and "furnishings" for ladies, gents and children.

1916

Community

Greensboro had four banks, and 33 churches representing 13 denominations, the city directory revealed. There were three social clubs: the Elks, the Merchants and Manufacturers, and the Country Club.

1918

Greensboro Record, c. 1934. *State Archives of North Carolina*

Journalism

E.B. Jeffress of Asheville, who had acquired an ownership stake in the *Daily News* seven years earlier, became the guiding force behind the newspaper when he added three associates to the staff — who bought out Walter Hildebrand's shares.

Hildebrand set one condition on the deal, however: that the paper would always be "kind" to Republicans.

The *Daily News*, however, leaned Democratic from that time forward, reflecting Jeffress' views. At the time, Greensboro had three competing newspapers: The *Daily News*, with offices at Davie and Market, the *Daily Record* at 201 West Market, and the *Patriot*, at 118½ North Elm.

The *Patriot* had been first on the scene, dating all the way back to 1869. The *Record*, which appeared in 1890, had been founded by a group of three printers who'd probably worked for the *Patriot* before that. One of them, Joseph Reece, bought out the other two and ran the newspaper until his death in 1915.

1919

Community

Arthur K. Wood laid out the middle-class neighborhood of Westerwood a mile west of downtown. ...

Charles Hudson developed the Arlington Park neighborhood.

Education

The State Normal and Industrial College changed its name to the North Carolina College for Women.

Lodging

The city's first modern hotel, the O. Henry, opened at North Elm and Bellemeade.

Plans for a $320,000 hotel to be named for the famous writer had been announced as far back as 1916, but as is often the case, the projected cost rose by the time construction got under way: The winning bid, announced in May of 1917, as for $435,000.

The O. Henry Hotel is seen at North Elm and Bellemeade streets in 1978, the year before it was demolished. *William Heroy, Historic American Building Survey, Library of Congress*

Excitement surrounding the project was such that the Scott Seed & Grocery Company announced it was introducing "O. Henry Hotel Blend Coffee." It was actually the same kind of coffee sold in other cities, but the company hoped the local name and a lower price (25 cents a pound compared to 30 cents elsewhere) would boost sales.

Featuring 300 rooms, the hotel was built through local stock subscriptions on the site where a home owned by Clement G. Wright once stood. A dedication ceremony was held July 2, with boyhood friends of O. Henry paying tribute to the writer as part of the program. The hotel was opened to the public from 2 to 5 in the afternoon before an evening banquet and dance in the O. Henry ballroom.

The hotel included a converted tobacco warehouse, which served as an annex to handle overflow guests and, for many years, remained popular with travelers visiting the city. In 1936, it was purchased by the Dinkler Hotels Co., which owned hotels in places like Nashville, Atlanta, Savannah, New Orleans, Birmingham, Jacksonville, and Louisville. At one point, it boasted more than 3,000 rooms.

But the O. Henry closed in the 1960s and demolished in 1979. The current O. Henry Hotel on Green Valley Road near the Friendly Center is a different structure entirely.

The O. Henry Hotel shortly before its demolition in 1978. *Historic American Building Survey, Library of Congress*

The original O. Henry Hotel ballroom, top, and lobby, above, as seen in 1978. *William Heroy, Historic American Building Survey, Library of Congress*

The new O. Henry Hotel on Green Valley Road. *Author photo*

Roaring Into the Twenties
1920–1929

The Guilford County Courthouse was built between 1918 and 1920.
Author photo

1920

Baseball

A new incarnation of the Greensboro Patriots took the field for the first season of the new Class-D Piedmont League, featuring five teams in North Carolina and one in southern Virginia.

The Patriots edged out the Raleigh Nats for the title by 2 games, posting a 69-51 record in the regular season, then beating them 4 games to 3 in the championship series.

Two Smiths — outfielder/shortstop Lloyd and catcher Herbert "Doc" Smith — both hit over .300, with Doc Smith slugging 16 homers. On the mound, rookie Ike Sadler enjoyed his best season with a 19-9 record and an earned-run average of 2.36.

The Piedmont League would step up to Class C the following season. The Patriots failed to repeat as regular-season champions, but won a playoff series against the second-place High Point Furniture Makers, 4 games to 1. First-place Raleigh did not participate in the postseason.

Unfortunately, the Cone Park grandstand burned after the third game of the playoff series, forcing fans to sit in temporary seating the rest of the way.

With the exception of 1922, the Patriots continued to finish near the top of the standings over the next few seasons.

Business

When the nine-story American Exchange National Bank Building opened at 100 Elm Street, it was the tallest building in Greensboro.

Two years in the making, it cost $300,000 to build.

The bank itself was the product of a 1911 merger between the American Exchange Bank and Commercial National Bank. Business operations for the bank were on the lower floors of the new building, with offices on the upper floors being rented out. It was so successful that an annex was added in 1927, creating an L-shaped complex.

But the bank, like so many others, was hit hard by the stock market crash of 1929. It was taken over by the North Carolina Bank and Trust Company, which in turn closed its doors on March 4, 1933, when President Franklin D. Roosevelt declared a bank holiday to create new regulations for the industry.

Just two banks opened their doors again afterward, but the North Carolina Bank and Trust stayed closed for good. The Southeastern Realty Company, which owned the building, sold it to Ben Cone, and it became known as the Southeastern Building.

Community

Guilford County was getting a new courthouse, and it wasn't the first time. Greensboro kept outgrowing its courthouses, and by the time 1915 rolled around, it had done so yet again: A new courthouse was needed, which would be the city's sixth. Architects envisioned a 10-story structure, but voters decided against the plan.

So a new plan emerged to build a courthouse at the center of a 300-foot town square called Courthouse Park.

The former courthouse square was sold to the Jefferson Standard Life Insurance Company in 1917, and it was renamed Jefferson Square five years after that. In the meantime, work on the new courthouse, facing West Market Street, began in 1918. A solid-looking Renaissance Revival structure with Greek ornamentation, it would measure 170 feet long by 74 feet wide.

Total cost: $750,000.

Milestones

Greensboro's population was on the cusp of 20,000 at 19,861 after adding almost exactly 5,000 people in the previous decade.

1921

The National Theatre. *elmorovivo, Creative Commons 2.0, cinematreasures*

Cinema

The new National Theatre boasted 1,800 seats and played host to vaudeville performances and touring Broadway shows like the original production of *Oklahoma!*, the stage version of *Harvey* with Joe E. Brown, and Noel Coward's *Private Lives*, with Tallulah Bankhead.

Elvis Presley played four shows — two matinees and a pair of evening shows — there in February 1956, but the National went into decline shortly after that. It shifted its focus from blockbusters to B movies around the late fifties, and was closed by 1966.

A year later it was demolished to make way for a parking lot.

Government

Claude Kiser began a two-year mayoral term.

1922

Development

A distinctive building, its shape dictated by an acute angle where Summit Avenue met Lindsay and Church streets, went up at the intersection. The four-unit apartment building was known as the Flatiron because of its shape.

The Studebaker and Cadillac dealerships. *Author photo*

Retail

Cadillac established a dealership in a two-story brick building at 304 East Market Street. A building in the same style for Studebaker was constructed right next door on what soon became an auto row, with Buick, Chrysler-Plymouth, and Chevrolet also setting up shop.

The Cadillac dealership was a branch of the Winston-Salem Carolina Cadillac Company, and the two-story showroom offered plenty of space. Initially, there were just four cars on display, and the dealership had just four employees: a salesman, two mechanics, and a janitor.

Buicks and Oldsmobiles were later sold there, too. It was at the center of a now-quiet neighborhood that was once a bustling collection of boarding houses, taverns, billiard parlors, and other businesses: places like Bishop's Record Shop (operating at Market and Davie in 1942) Cox Furniture, Harold Sykes' Amoco station, the New Baltimore Café at 252 East Market, and Weinstein Music at 201 South Davie.

The dealership would move to a new showroom on Bessemer in 1966.

1923

Business

The new Jefferson Standard Building, a skyscraper 18 stories high, was completed at the corner of Elm and Market streets.

When first announced back in 1920, it was only projected to be 12 stories tall, but its scope grew as planning progressed. By April of the following year, plans were calling for a 15-story skyscraper.

When complete, the structure easily eclipsed the

American Exchange Bank's nine-story building as the city's tallest, and for four years (until the Nissen Building went up in Winston-Salem), it was the tallest building between Atlanta and Washington, D.C.

Built by the Jefferson Standard Insurance Company, the building — like the company — was named for Thomas Jefferson, whose bust appeared above the entrance.

Company president Julian Price steered the project to completion, and Jefferson Standard clearly had no trouble

The Jefferson Standard Building in 2022.
Author photo

paying for it: The $177,000 paid for the land and the $2.5 million it cost to build the skyscraper were both paid in cash.

The insurance company's offices occupied just the first five floors of the high-rise, with the ground floor also housing a tobacconist, barber, florist, and jeweler among other retail stores, along with a railway ticket office. With 129 businesses and 1,000 employees working there, it was considered a "city within a city."

Community

Greensboro annexed the Lindley Park, College Park, and McAdoo Heights neighborhoods, along with Scott Park, College Heights, and East Side Park in the Jonesboro area around the Negro Agricultural and Technical College of North Carolina (later North Carolina A&T).

1924

Community

The Greensboro Carnegie Negro Library took a long time to become reality.

It was first conceived back in 1905, when Andrew Carnegie offered $10,000 to build a segregated library. He'd already donated $30,000 for the city's first Carnegie Library after the city applied for funds back around 1902, and it had been completed four years later.

But it took the city's second Carnegie Library nearly two decades to become reality. Debate over just where it should be built delayed construction, with Bennett College offering a site on its campus in 1916. But opponents argued it shouldn't be placed on private land.

Nevertheless, the 2,000-square-foot building eventually was completed there and opened in October of 1924 with a small collection of 150 volumes. By 1930, however, it had the largest circulation of any segregated public library in the state.

The Greensboro Carnegie Negro Library. *Author photo*

Demand became such that the initially small collection outgrew its home, with 28,000 volumes packed into the small building. The library merged with the city's library system in 1963, six years after Greensboro's libraries were integrated, and closed three years later. Unlike the city's first Carnegie library, it remains standing, having been converted into offices for Bennett College.

Faith

A new synagogue opened on Greene Street, serving 75 Jewish families in Greensboro.

1925

Community

The Hamtown neighborhood, named for grocer Joseph Ham, was being developed three miles north of downtown. ...

The Rankin neighborhood was subdivided. The area three miles northeast of downtown would be annexed into the city of Greensboro less than a decade later. Most of the houses built there were bungalows, lining streets laid out in an irregular, sometimes curvilinear pattern.

Government

E.B. Jeffress was elected mayor, serving until 1927. Jeffress, a Democrat, was also a newspaper publisher and later served on the North Carolina House of Representatives from 1931 to 1933.

1926

The entrance to World War Memorial Stadium. *Author photo*

Athletics

World War Memorial Stadium was dedicated on Armistice Day on a 14-acre site donated by the Cone family at 510 Yanceyville Street.

Originally designed to seat 25,000 fans, the plans were scaled back, and the stadium opened with seating for 8,500 and room for 4,000 more bleacher seats. A canopy, press box, and dugouts would be added in 1930 with the arrival of the Greensboro Patriots baseball team.

Two views inside World War Memorial Stadium, and crossed bats (inset) near the entrance outside. *Author photos*

Aerial view of World War Memorial Stadium. *State Archives of North Carolina*

Two bronze plaques bearing the names of 80 men who had died in World War I were unveiled at ceremonies that began at 10:30 a.m. Those who had gathered for the occasion then went inside and listened to speeches by Mayor Edwin Jeffress, and U.S. Rep. Alfred Bulwinkle, a veteran of the war.

A football game followed, matching High Point and Guilford colleges, with High Point winning a low-scoring affair, 7-3.

In addition to hosting the Greensboro Patriots baseball team, the stadium would serve as home to successive minor-league teams over the years, as well as the Greensboro Red Wings Negro League team in the late 1940s and the North Carolina A&T ballclub (which still played there as of 2021).

The college's football teams also called the stadium home until Aggie Stadium opened in 1981.

Baseball

The Greensboro Patriots captured the Piedmont League pennant with an 86-60 mark, then defeated the Durham Bulls 4 games to 1 in a playoff series.

The Patriots had a potent lineup, with Dave Barbee socking a league-leading 29 homers and Molly Cox adding 22. Fair Crews (yes, that was his real name) led the pitching staff with a 19-5 record and a 2.65 ERA. Each of the six pitchers on the staff posted a winning record.

The Carolina Theatre under construction in 1926. *CarolinaTD, Creative Commons 2.0, cinematreasures*

Cinema

Ground was broken July 21 on the new Carolina Theatre downtown.

It cost more than half a million dollars to build.

Community

First Realty and Loan of Greensboro laid out the Highland Park West neighborhood. Many residents worked in the surrounding mills, including the Pomona Cotton Mill and the Mock, Judson, Voehringer Hosiery Mill.

Greensboro would annex the neighborhood in 1956.

David D. Jones Student Union at Bennett College. *Author photo*

Education

Bennett College, founded in 1874, was reorganized as a women's college.

Fire

A new fire station opened downtown on Greene Street with six arched bays.

Sedgefield Country Club. *Author photo*

Golf

Sedgefield Country Club, which would frequently play host to the Greater Greensboro Open beginning in 1938, opened about midway between Greensboro and High Point. Former British Open champion Walter Hagen was quoted as saying "it has every prospect of being an excellent course."

Non-resident membership was $300, with a discount of $25 for cash payments, and there were no dues on what was described in ads as "practically a life membership."

Radio

Greensboro had its first radio station, WNRC. The station went on the air May 2, operating out of the Jefferson Standard Building. The state's tallest building at the time, it was the perfect place to mount a transmission tower.

The station changed its call letters in 1930 to WBIG, for "We Believe in Greensboro," but it suffered a devastating blow when the tower was destroyed by a lightning strike in 1934 and went bankrupt.

Jefferson Standard Life Insurance bought the station for $10,000. It became a CBS affiliate, with its studios moving to the basement of the O. Henry Hotel.

As of 1939, it was on the air from 6:30 a.m. to midnight under the management of Edney Ridge. Under station policy, it did not advertise wine or liquor, and made it clear that certain things were not permitted: things like "exalting gangsters, criminals and racketeers; disrespect for parents or other proper authority; cruelty, greed, and selfishness as worthy motivations" or "programs that arouse harmful or nervous reactions in a child."

Also, "conceit, smugness or an unwarranted sense of superiority over others less fortunate may not be presented as laudable."

1927

Charles Lindbergh speaks at World War Memorial Stadium.
State Archives of North Carolina

Aviation

Lindley Field was established, with 12,000 people turning out for the dedication ceremony.

The airfield was officially called Tri-County Airport but was popularly known as Lindley Field after Paul Lindley, a prominent business owner who had sold the land where it was built to the city and Guilford County. (Lindley was also a city council member and future mayor.)

The airfield was one of just two stops in North Carolina on Charles Lindbergh's three-month national tour on the heels of his New York-to-Paris flight in May. The famous aviator — who visited 82 cities in all — arrived overhead around 11:22 on October 14 and circled several times before landing his *Spirit of St. Louis* at 11:29 a.m.

There he was greeted by Governor A.W. McLean and the mayors of Greensboro and High Point. But within minutes he was quickly whisked away in a convertible, riding through the city in a motorcade to World War Memorial Stadium, where he appeared and gave a brief talk before a cheering crowd.

It was a whirlwind tour: He was scheduled to be in Winston-Salem by 2 p.m.

Business

The 13-story Greensboro Bank and Trust Building was completed at 301 South Elm Street. It was the second-tallest building in Greensboro upon completion, trailing only the Jefferson Standard Building — which had been designed by the same architect, Charles Hartmann.

The building, which took slightly more than a year to complete, was a new home for the bank, which had been around since 1899.

With construction costs penciling out to $900,000, it featured the kind of luxurious feel that had become a staple of major banking establishments at the time, including a marble, bronze, and walnut banking room.

The Greensboro Bank and Trust Building was the second tallest in Greensboro upon its completion in 1927. *Author photo*

Cinema

The Carolina Theatre, dubbed "The Showplace of the Carolinas," opened at 310 South Greene Street. It was the largest in the state with 2,200 seats: 1,300 on the orchestra floor and 900 more in the balconies.

The Carolina was emblematic of the "movie palaces" that opened during the Roaring Twenties, when the nation was flush with money to spend on entertainment. It looked from the front like a Roman temple.

Top: The Carolina during a showing of the 1930 film *Blotto*, featuring Laurel and Hardy. *Granola, Creative Commons 2.0, cinematreasures*
Above: Carolina Theatre lobby, 1949. *CarolinaTD, Creative Commons 2.0, cinematreasures*

The Carolina Theatre in 2022. *Author photos*

The ceiling of the ornate main lobby was painted blue and pink to look like a twilight sky. A chandelier hung from the ceiling, and a row of green marble columns lined the mezzanine behind and above the concession stand.

In the auditorium, another crystal chandelier hung from an oval dome. And the stage was equally impressive at 90 feet high and 35 feet deep, large enough to accommodate not only vaudeville acts but circus performers.

Community

The town of Hamilton Lakes began was taking shape, with streets, residential lots, a golf course, and two lakes. Alfred M. Scales, who had helped develop the Irving Park neighborhood, laid out the new town, building an 11,000-square-foot home of his own lakeside. He served as the town's first mayor.

Government

R.R. King began a two-year term as mayor.

The Christian Advocate building on West Friendly Avenue in 2022. *Author photo*

Journalism

The Christian Advocate Publishing Company moved into a new two-story building at 427 West Friendly Avenue. Its Egyptian Revival architecture featured lotus-design relief columns on both ends of the front, built with heavy cast stone.

The Hotel King Cotton towers above Greensboro in this photo from 1954.

Lodging

Cotton broker J.E. Latham built the 300-room Hotel King Cotton at East Market and Davie streets, now the site of a multilevel parking structure.

The once-majestic hotel was eventually converted into a dormitory for North Carolina A&T students, who created new problems there.

It was finally imploded in the early 1970s.

Transportation

A new depot, the most impressive ever built in North Carolina, opened on East Washington Street.

The J. Douglas Galyon Depot was the work of a New York company that made its reputation designing train stations. And that reputation could only have been enhanced by this, its latest project. A neoclassical temple to trains with six thick columns out front, its arched entrance led to an interior with wooden benches that had room for 1,000 passengers.

About 90 trains came and went each day at the depot in the Gate City, which had already earned that nickname because of its rail traffic and central location in the Piedmont.

The depot replaced the previous station at 400 South Elm. When it eventually closed in 1979, an Amtrak train was the only one that stopped there.

Greensboro Station, completed in 1927.
Author photo

Weather

March 3 brought snow, and a lot of it. A total of 20 inches fell, setting a city record that still stood almost a century later. That provided the bulk of the 32.5 inches of snow for the year, which also set a record.

1928

Aviation

Regular air mail service started out of Lindley Field.

Community

The Kirkwood subdivision was laid out on what had formerly been farmland owned by David Kirkpatrick. ...

The cornerstone was set for a new Masonic Temple at 424 West Market Street, near the home of O. Henry (William Sidney Porter).

It was no ordinary cornerstone.

The stone, which measured 24 inches by 42 inches by 12 inches was brought all the way from King Solomon's Quarries in Jerusalem.

Greensboro architect John B. Crawford, who designed the building, received a missive detailing the difficulties of procuring the desired stone:

"The men worked at it for a very long time, until the piece was almost disengaged; then without warning, it cracked and fell over on the ground, just escaping falling on one of the quarriers," the letter read.

"As the crack took off the corner, this piece had to be abandoned and a new one sought. The second entailed much more work than the first; but it finally was ready to be put on the back of an exceptionally strong camel who had been trained to work in the eternal night of Solomon's Quarries."

Construction started on January 14, and the cornerstone was set on March 20.

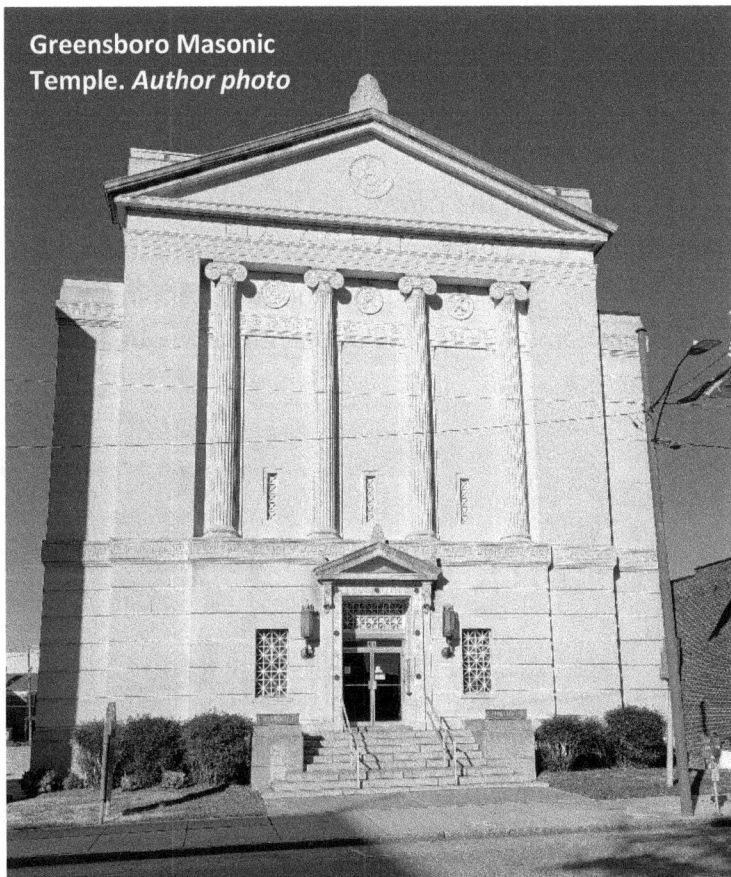

Greensboro Masonic Temple. *Author photo*

Retail

Montgomery Ward opened another store in its growing chain, setting up shop on East Market Street. The company had gotten its start running a mail-order catalog business back in 1872, but it hadn't opened its first retail outlet until 1926. Growth came quickly after that: The Greensboro store was the 100th in the chain.

1929

Bowling

A certificate of incorporation was filed with the secretary of state's office to operate a public bowling center in Greensboro. The 1930 city directory listed Greensboro Bowling Alleys operating at 355 North Elm Street, with G.B. Winslow serving as manager.

A few years later, the Downtown Bowling Alley would open for "duck pin" bowling at 111 East Washington Street. (Duckpin bowling uses smaller balls and squatter pins than the similar ten-pin game.) You could play at either venue for a quarter a game.

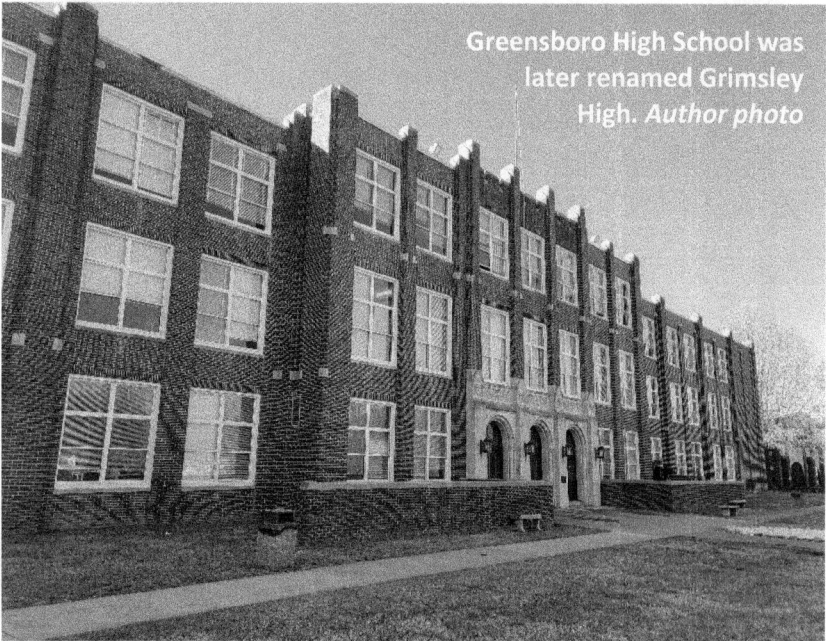

Greensboro High School was later renamed Grimsley High. *Author photo*

Education

Greensboro High School, founded in 1899, moved to a new $1 million campus on Westover Terrace that looked more like a college than a high school. The school would be renamed

Grimsley High in 1962 to honor former public-school superintendent Adonijah Grimsley.

Fast Food

Boar & Castle opened at 3907 West Market Street, serving up fries or onion rings alongside its signature Castleburger. The drive-in would remain open until 1980.

Retail

The new building at 132 South Elm Street would be home to the city's new F.W. Woolworth five-and-dime store.

The downtown six-bay fire station was completed in 1926. The 12-story Marriott Greensboro Downtown Hotel was a later addition, rising behind it in 1984. *Author photo*

Elm Street at Market near the old courthouse, c. 1920s. *State Archives of North Carolina*

The Flatiron building, a four-unit wedge-shaped apartment building, went up in 1922. *Author photo*

The first passenger plane leaves Greensboro on Nov. 6, 1930, with passengers below. *State Archives of North Carolina*

Survive to Thrive

1930–1939

The new S.H. Kress Building went up downtown in 1930.
Author photo

1930

Baseball

The Greensboro Patriots played their first game at World War Memorial Stadium on April 24, later taking the field for their first night game on July 18.

The ballclub teamed up with the Cardinals to become a St. Louis affiliate in the team. (Branch Rickey, the major league team's manager and later executive, pioneered farm club affiliations.)

Golf

Starmount Forest Golf Club, designed by Wayne Stiles and John Van Kleek, opened August 1 on West Market Street. A golf shop and ballroom would be added late in the decade, along with a kitchen and dining room. Later additions included four tennis courts and, in 1956, a swimming pool.

Journalism

The *Greensboro Daily News* purchased the rival *Record*, although the two papers continued for some time as separate entities, one publishing in the morning and the other in the afternoon.

Milestones

Greensboro's population had exploded in the 1920s, rising from less than 20,000 to a whopping 53,569 by 1930, an increase of nearly 170 percent.

Retail

S.H. Kress was a chain of five-and-dime stores, but the front of the new building at 212 South Elm Street looked like it belonged on a swanky department store or a movie palace.

Designed by architect Edward Sibbert, a graduate of Cornell University, the four-story building was the work of G.A. Miller from Tampa. Miller was clearly proud of the finished product:

"Of the new Kress Greensboro store, it may be sincerely said that there is no finer building of its kind in the world," he stated. "It is a distinct addition to the business center of the city and a store of which Greensboro may be proud."

Unlike department stores, which frequently used multiple floors for sales space, the Kress store confined displays to the ground floor. A lunch room and offices occupied the second floor, with the upper two floors reserved for storage.

Two views of a heavy snowstorm in 1930. *State Archives of North Carolina*

1931

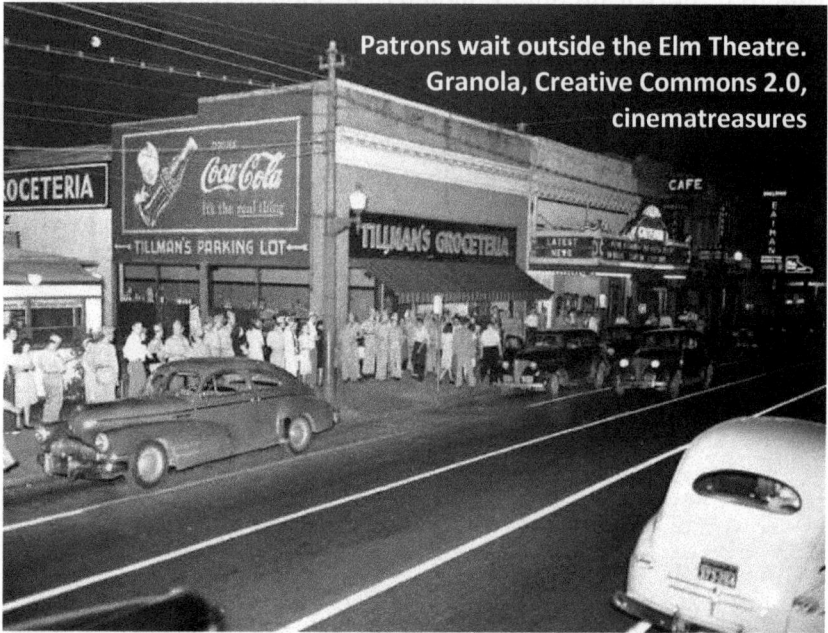

Patrons wait outside the Elm Theatre. Granola, Creative Commons 2.0, cinematreasures

Cinema

It would go by three different names over the course of more than three decades, but the movie house at 220 North Elm Street started out as the Paramount Theatre when it opened in 1931. As many as 1,800 spectators could fit into its single auditorium, with adults paying 20 cents for a ticket and children admitted for a dime.

Just a year after it opened, the Paramount became the Criterion. In 1933, it charged 10 cents for matinees and 15 cents for evening showings of a movie called *The Painted Woman*, starring Spencer Tracey and Peggy Shannon. The matinees were for "ladies only," while only men were allowed for the night screenings. No one under 16 was admitted.

In 1948, the theater's name was changed again, this time to the Elm. It had undergone renovations and was now being hailed as "Greensboro's most modern theatre."

It would operate as the Elm until it closed in the mid-1960s. The cinema was eventually demolished.

Government

Paul Lindley was elected mayor.

1932

Education

The North Carolina College for Women underwent another name change: Now it was the Woman's College of the University of North Carolina.

1933

Baseball

The Greensboro Patriots were the class of the Piedmont League (which had moved up to Class B the previous season), compiling a 90-48 record and outpacing second-place Charlotte by 11½ games.

The pitching staff boasted three 20-game winners in Johnny Chambers, Virgil Brown, and Dykes Potter, along with the league's most feared hitter. Jim Bucher hit .369 while leading the league in hits (188), doubles (40) and home runs (25). He would go on to play eight major-league seasons with the Dodgers, Cardinals, and Red Sox.

But despite all that, he wasn't the biggest name on the roster in 1933.

That was another future major-leaguer.

Johnny Mize had made his debut with the Patriots in 1930 and had batted just .194, but had improved to .337 the following year before spending a season in Elmira Red Birds up in New York. He was back for a third season with the Patriots in 1933 and had by far the best season of his minor-league career, socking 22 homers to go with a .360 average and 29 doubles.

Patriots team photo and an unidentified player in the early 1930s. State Archives of North Carolina

His performance got him promoted to Double-A Rochester, and he was in the majors with the Cardinals by 1936. During a 15-year big-league career, he batted .312 with 359 home runs, including 51 with the New York Giants in 1947. He surpassed 100 RBI eight times in a nine-season stretch, was a 10-time All-Star, and was elected to the Hall of Fame in 1981.

Unfortunately for the Patriots, they were unable to defend

their league championship. With Mize and Bucher both gone, they plummeted from first to worst in the Piedmont League in 1935, which turned out to be their final season. Greensboro wouldn't field another minor-league team until just before World War II.

A new post office and U.S. courthouse, built for more than half a million dollars, was dedicated in 1933. *Author photo*

Community

Some 4,000 people showed up in July to see a new post office and courthouse dedicated on West Market Street. U.S. Postmaster General James Farley attended, along with Senators Robert Reynolds and Josiah Bailey.

The building, constructed from granite, limestone, and aluminum, cost roughly $585,000 to build. It was the first structure in Greensboro to be built in the art deco/streamline moderne style.

Milestones

Mayor Paul Lindley died in a freak accident, falling overboard from a fishing boat on his farm and drowning in water just 7 feet deep.

It wasn't that Lindley didn't know how to swim. But he'd recently dislocated his arm and, as a result, was unable to save himself.

Lindley had spent eight years on the city council, the last two as mayor, but he'd been a major civic presence before that as head of the J. Van Lindley Nursery and director of Jefferson Standard Life Insurance.

Roger W. Harrison served the next four years as mayor before resigning.

Where cars spent the night

The Greensboro Auto Inn at 235 Commerce Place is seen here during the early 1930s. It advertised itself as "Greensboro's only fireproof auto inn." You could buy Sinclair brand gasoline and motor oil, get your car washed, or have it stored. It was open "day & night." *State Archives of North Carolina*

1934

Greensboro residents turn out for Armistice Day and Christmas parades in the early 1930s. *State Archives of North Carolina*

Community

The City Directory showed Greensboro encompassing 18.4 square miles, including 401.6 acres in 17 parks. There were 292 miles of streets, although less than half of those miles (137) were paved.

You wouldn't have any trouble finding a telephone, because there were 7,900 of them. And people of faith could choose among 73 churches in 22 denominations.

Even amid the Depression, there were still people working: More than 8,300 people had jobs at 101 manufacturing plants. There were two daily newspapers to read, a radio station to listen to, and two "Class A" hotels with 900 rooms. As far as entertainment went, there were eight movie theaters and three golf courses.

There were plenty of schools, too: 19 public schools with 13,000 students and 278 teachers. Add to that four institutions of higher learning and a couple of libraries containing nearly 40,000 volumes.

1935

Cinema

The State Theatre opened November 25 with seating for 500 at 331 South Elm Street. It would remain open for 20 years.

Retail

Greensboro had plenty of choices when it came to grocery shopping, including eight Piggly Wiggy locations and seven Ivory stores.

The Ivory chain, owned by the Irvin Wholesale Grocery Company of Greensboro, claimed to sell "fancy groceries" in "Greensboro's cleanest and lowest-priced food stores." They were "self-service stores of the highest type, with fresh meat markets, all over the city."

Owner and founder Charles W. Irvin had moved to Greensboro around 1924, and the first Ivory Store had appeared by 1928 or earlier at 108 West Market Street. There were four Ivories by 1930, with Irvin stocking (among other items) more than 100 Libby food products.

"Up to four years ago we stocked a number of brands of canned foods," he said. "But our turnover was small and our inventory showed too much dead stock. Then we began to handle Libby Foods in a small way. We finally discontinued all unadvertised brands and stocked up with Libby's — over 100 different items. We've had a fine increase in volume."

That testimonial appeared in a promotional piece for Libby's in *The Progressive Grocer* from 1930. Whether because of Libby's popularity or for some other reason, Ivory Stores prospered for a while. Irvin was even elected president of the Greensboro Merchants' Association in 1933.

There were still six Ivory Stores in Greensboro in 1940, and two locations remained open as late as 1960. One of those was at 3006 West Gate City Boulevard, and the other was at 612 Walker Avenue.

The latter was the longest lasting Ivory Store, opening around 1935 and staying open for about a quarter-century. The Art Deco building is still there today.

The Ivory Store at 612 Walker Avenue as it appeared on a vintage postcard.

The building that once housed the Ivory Store at 612 Walker Avenue, seen in 2022. *Author photo*

The Ivory chain — which drew the inspiration for its name from the stores' white fixtures — even ventured beyond Greensboro, opening a store on Main Street in Burlington in 1934 that featured the "wait-on-yourself-and-save-the-difference" system.

Charles W. Irvin died of a heart attack in 1960 at the age of 64, and shortly after that, the chain was no more.

If Ivory stuck around a while, the same couldn't be said for another chain, W&M Stores. Five stores were open in 1935, but they'd all disappeared by 1940.

Transportation

U.S. Highway 220 was extended south through town.

1936

Weather

The first tornado in Greensboro history was a doozy. What

the *Burlington Daily Times-News* called a "freak twister" struck in early April, causing more than $1.5 million in damage. The initial count showed at least a dozen people dead and more than 100 injured.

The death toll eventually reached 14, making it the second-deadliest in state history.

Sheets of tin roofing hung from tree limbs and wires. Pieces of wood flung violently about by the storm lodged themselves in homes that were otherwise unscathed.

The twister barreled through the south side of Greensboro south of downtown. The hardest-hit area was the 400 block of Gorrell Street, where just one in eight of the buildings remained on its foundation.

The rest were destroyed.

"It was a horrible sight to see them drag my sister's body from the ruins of that house" at 406 Gorrell, said Mrs. H.M. Raper, who was at work when the twister hit. "I don't know where my husband is. I haven't seen him since yesterday when the tornado struck."

1937

Retail

The supermarket era arrived in Greensboro with the opening of the Pender Grocery Co.'s first Big Star location, downtown at Washington and Greene streets. It was Pender's first supermarket, sometimes referred to as "Pender's Yellow Front" instead of Big Star.

Other Big Star supermarkets soon followed in places like High Point and Winston-Salem.

1938

Golf

The first Greater Greensboro Open was a memorable one, as Sam Snead posted a score of 271 over four rounds, a new low for a major tournament.

He beat Johnny Revolta by five strokes.

The win at the Sedgefield Country Club and Starmount Forest courses earned Snead $1,200, but it was just the beginning for the West Virginia native.

Snead would go on to win the tourney seven more times — in 1946, 1949, 1950, 1955, 1956, 1960, and 1965. His widest margin of victory came in '50, when he won by a whopping 10 strokes, shooting 11 under par. No other golfer won the tourney more than twice in the 20th century.

A & P PRESENTS—
Greensboro's
Newest and Largest
Food Store

FOOD A&P STORE
SELF SERVICE

A newspaper ad for the new A&P supermarket.

Retail

Big Star opened the city's first supermarket, and A&P was not far behind.

A&P had long operated as a corner grocer, with thousands of locations across the country — including 18 in Greensboro by 1935. The company had resisted opening larger locations, but by this time, the writing was on the wall: It would have to adapt.

With this in mind, A&P opened its first Greensboro supermarket, an 11,000-square-foot store in an old tobacco warehouse at 225 Commerce Place. It was the largest A&P between Washington and Atlanta.

Two years later, A&P had closed half of the 18 smaller stores that had been open in the city just five years before. Most of the shuttered locations were within a couple of miles of downtown. ...

A&P opened a corner market at what is now 747 West Gate City Boulevard in 1925, above, then moved to a larger store, top, at 901 West Gate City in 1928. *Author photos*

Two other early A&P stores opened in the Lindley Park area in 1930, top, and at Glenwood and Grove, above. The latter store was closed by 1935 and later became a Bi-Rite location. *Author photos*

The former Montgomery Ward store, at right, Elm Street today. Next door is the Vernon Building, the oldest building downtown, which dates to 1883 and once housed a W.T. Grant. A demolished building farther left was home to a Belk Department store. *Author photo*

The Vernon Building is seen at left, beyond the now-vanished Belk Building, in this photo from the 1930s. *State Archives of North Carolina*

Montgomery Ward moved to a new, three-story building with 35,000 square feet of space at 230-232 South Elm Street downtown, marking the new store with "M.W." on the tiled entrance and a "W" at the top of the building front.

Ward was just one of several department stores on the block, with discount chain W.T. Grant on one side and Efird's having opened on the other side just a week earlier. Belk was also on the 200 block, along with local entries Ellis-Stone and Meyer's. Sears was right around the corner on Greene.

Ward would stay in that location for 22 years before closing in 1957. The chain, which had begun as a catalog house, wouldn't return to Greensboro for nearly two decades, opening a store at the new Carolina Circle Mall in 1976.

That store would remain open until 2001, when it and the only other remaining Montgomery Ward in North Carolina, in Asheville, both closed along with nearly 250 other Wards stores and the company went out of business.

South Elm near Sycamore in the 1930s. At left is the Whelan Drug Company, occupying a space in the Woolworth Building later filled by the Jewel Box and Carlyle & Co. *State Archives of North Carolina*

1939

The Oden Brewing Company building in 2022. *Author photo*

Business

William Lafayette Oden opened a soda brewing company at what's now 804 Gate City Boulevard, in a building he constructed for $2,000. There, Oden produced a beverage he dubbed Three-Centa, a carbonated soft drink that, unfortunately, failed to take off.

No matter. He tried again, this time with a ginger ale he called Buffalo Rock; the company remained in operation until 1963.

Government

Ralph L. Lewis became mayor but served for just one year before resigning.

Radio

Charlie Monroe's program on WBIG radio featured a fellow called String Bean — real name David Akeman — who played the banjo.

Akeman would go on to perform at the Grand Ole Opry and, in 1969, became a regular on the new syndicated TV show *Hee Haw*. Sadly, he was and his wife were shot and killed at their home in 1973 by two burglars who had ambushed them when they returned from a performance at the Opry.

Retail

Mitchell's Clothing opened its doors at 311 East Market Street downtown.

It was founded by John Mitchell's father and uncle in 1939, and Mitchell himself started helping out there after school when he was 11 or 12 because "I was forced into it," he joked in a 2022 interview for this book.

Before that, when he was about 9 years old, he sold peanuts at Patriots baseball games. "Back then, you had to work," he said. "If you walked, you worked."

He was still working at the age of 94, having taken over from his father in 1962 — six full decades ago. Until then, the store specialized in heavy-duty clothes for mill workers. But when Mitchell bought his father out, he shifted his inventory toward "high fashion," selling things like platform shoes, leisure suits, and a wide selection of fancy hats from makers like Stetson and Kangol.

He described his merchandise as "medium-priced dress clothes: I'm a step ahead of Kmart and Walmart, and maybe a half-step behind Belk."

Mitchell's, foreground, and the Dabbs Furniture building. *Author photo*

During the interview, a customer came in wanting a hat that looked "superfly." The hats took up a large section near the center of the store. Mitchell's reply: "If you don't see it, we ain't got it." Mitchell's wry sense of humor was on display throughout the interview.

He claims to have sold the first pair of bell bottoms in Greensboro. And he even sold the same low-cut shirt made famous by singer Tom Jones.

Mitchell's stayed open as other businesses in the neighborhood came and went. There was the Cadillac showroom across the street, a Hudson dealership, Greensboro Barbecue, the Clegg-King barbershop.

Until the early 1970s, guests at the King Cotton Hotel might have stopped in occasionally. The 13-story hotel was just a city block down Market Street until it was demolished.

"It was a nice hotel," Mitchell recalled. "They had a barbershop and a couple of stores up there. One reason they tore it down was some students moved in and started throwing bottles down onto the street."

But back in the day, it was a vibrant neighborhood.

"The *Daily News* used to be right up the street," Mitchell recalled. "Down on hamburger circle, they used to have Jim's Diner and another diner." There were several pool rooms, a pawn shop, a market called Joe's, an Esso filling station next door to his shop, and a train station in the neighborhood.

"They used to have rowhouses down there" by the train station, he said. "People would get off the train, stay the night and move on."

A Greek family lived upstairs next door to Mitchell's at 313 East Market, over Dabbs Furniture, which Mitchell recalled opened around 1949. Dick's Laundry, which opened back in the 1920s, was at Market and Lydon. Down Lydon just a short ways are two homes that date from 1905, one of which has been subdivided to create apartments.

"Duke Power used to be right next door," he said. "They used to make Coke right here on Fortis Street" (Church street).

A section of the 400 block, built in 1951, was the Eat Well Café and Guilford Cleaners. Just beyond is a railroad underpass — with smaller tunnels on either side that were designated for

Black and white pedestrians during segregation. It marked the gateway to the other side of the tracks, Mitchell said.

"The bridge was the dividing line. This was like the end zone."

The bridge on East Market Street marked a dividing line of sorts between two neighborhoods. *Author photo*

In a 2017 interview with *O. Henry Magazine*, Mitchell recalled diners that operated out of boxcars, a seafood place that had fresh fish on ice, brought in from the coast on Fridays. When he was very young, during Prohibition, he'd see businessmen and lawyers crossing the street and rounding the corner onto Lydon Street. He later learned that a bootlegger lived over on Lydon, and they went there to have some whiskey before heading back to work.

John Mitchell became such an institution that he came to be known as the "mayor of East Market Street." ...

A new Belt Department Store opened at Elm and Market, just down the street from the Hotel King Cotton. The four-story Art Deco Belk was the first air-conditioned store in the chain.

The Belk Department Store at Elm and Market is seen during its grand opening. *State Archives of North Carolina*

Greensboro as seen from the of the original O. Henry Hotel in the mid- to late 1930s. *State Archives of North Carolina*

Automobile service in 1930s Greensboro: Gate City Service Station was in business at 132 Asheboro, top, and Watson Stabilator Company operated at 224 East Sycamore during the 1930s. *State Archives of North Carolina*

A police officer directs traffic in Greensboro in, 1938. *John Vachon, Library of Congress*

<u>Wartime and Playtime</u>

1940-1949

Greensboro from the air, date unknown. *State Archives of North Carolina*

1940

Government

Huger King began a year in office as mayor.

Milestones

The Great Depression put a damper on Greensboro's growth, which dipped to less than 11 percent during the 1930s as the population rose to 59,319 in 1940.

1941

Baseball

The Greensboro Red Sox began a two-season run in the Piedmont League, managed by Hall of Fame outfielder Heinie Manush both years.

Manush's success on the field seemed to carry over in the dugout. During his first season at the helm, the Red Sox finished third with a 71-66 record and advance to the playoffs, beating the second-place Portsmouth Cubs 4 games to 2 in the semifinals before being swept by the pennant-winning Durham Bulls.

The following season was even better: The Red Sox finished first in the standings at 78-53, then swept the Charlotte Hornets in the playoffs and turned back Portsmouth 4 games to 2 for the championship.

Pitcher John Ostrowski led the league in wins, posting a 21-8 record in his best minor-league season. He later pitched five seasons in the American League with the St. Louis Browns and New York Yankees.

But despite their success, Boston transferred its affiliation to Roanoke, which replaced Greensboro in the league lineup the following year.

Cinema

The Drive-In was ahead of its time. Maybe that's why they just called it "The Drive-In." There weren't many others around when it opened: The first patented drive-in opened had opened less than a decade earlier, on June 6, 1933, in New Jersey.

The Drive-In was open Thursday, Friday and Saturday nights. If you paid a mere 30 cents, you could take one of the

600 spaces in front of the screen. "Children and cars" were free, and you could "smoke, chat, dress as you please."

Drive-ins didn't really take off until after the war, though, which meant The Drive-In on High Point Road — at what's now 3900 Gate City Boulevard — had the market all to itself. That lasted until 1949, when the North Drive-In opened on U.S. 29 at the opposite end of town. Then, to distinguish itself, it changed its name to (naturally) the South Drive-In.

Ad for the opening of The Drive-In on High Point Road.

Jim Bellows, who owned the downtown Center Theater, bought it in 1961, modernizing it: He added air conditioning to the restrooms and concession stand, installing new sound and projection equipment at the same time.

It closed in 1975 and was subsequently demolished.

1942

Community

The annual city directory declared Greensboro to be both "The City of Charm" and "Pivot of the Piedmont." Its principal products were denim, flannel, overalls, silk and cotton hose, cigars, fertilizer, pajamas, machinery, elastics, building tile, and sewer pipe. The city had:

- 19 parks with a total of 425 acres
- More than 15,000 telephones
- 122 churches representing 21 denominations
- 2 daily and 2 weekly newspapers
- 5 hospitals with 350 beds
- 14 hotels with 1,000 rooms
- 3 public libraries
- 25,176 workers in 252 industrial and service industries

Cinema

With World War II raging, the word "victory" seemed to be everywhere — including on Greensboro's newest theater. The movie house at 326 Tate Street, south of West Market, housed 1,100 and operated as the Victory Theater until 1958, when it became the Cinema Theatre.

It later became Janus Wings, when it was purchased by the owner of the Janus Theatre in 1977, and College Hill Cinema three years later. Still later, it was transformed into a hybrid pizza parlor and movie theater, where patrons could eat pizza while they watched movies.

The House of Pizza-Cinema lasted until the mid-1980s. The building later housed the Adams Book Store.

Government

W.H. Sullivan began a one-year stint as mayor.

1943

Army Air Force Overseas Replacement Depot, main entrance, 1944.

Military

In March, Greensboro became the site of the nation's largest military base within any city limits. The Army Air Force Basic Training Center No. 10 was built on a 652-acre site that welcomed 87,500 trainees for four to eight weeks of drills, along with weapons and chemical warfare training.

Women's Air Corps trainees were there for six weeks, and African Americans trained on the site as well (although it was segregated).

1944

Military

The Army Air Force Basic Training Center became the service's main Overseas Replacement Depot (ORD) for the East

Coast. Instead of training new AAF soldiers for deployment, it processed personnel for rotation overseas.

1945

Baseball

The Greensboro Patriots were back. Again. Or at least the name was.

This version of the Patriots played in the Class C Carolina League, where they finished dead last with a record of 53-83 and drew an average of just 765 fans to their games.

They'd do much better the following season, both on the field and at the gate. The Pats went from worst to first with an 85-57 record and drew an average of 2,420 fans a game to World War Memorial Stadium, although they fell to the Durham Bulls in a six-game postseason series.

The Patriots mostly finished in the bottom half of the standings for the rest of their time in the Carolina League, although they managed to place third in their final season, 1957. Greensboro's team was called the Yankees starting in 1958, but despite their connection to the most storied franchise in the majors, the Greensboro Yankees never won a pennant.

The Patriots name reappeared for a brief encore in 1968, by which time the Carolina League had moved up to Class A, but the team finished under .500 at 61-79 while averaging 378 fans a game. It wasn't enough to sustain them, and the Patriots were gone again the next season.

Government

C.M. Vanstory Jr. began a two-year term as mayor.

Military

The Army Air Force (ORD) began processing and discharging soldiers returning from overseas in September.

1946

Fast Food

The era of the drive-in kicked off right after World War II, and Bob Petty was ready.

He capitalized on the coming craze by setting up a white cinderblock building with green trim next door to his house on High Point Road. Inside, patrons could sit at a counter or booths, and could order menu items featured at the nearby Dixie Pig barbecue stop that had just closed. Outside were hot-rodders showing off their muscle cars.

Petty's was hardly the only drive-in around. Others included Monroe's on East Bessemer, the Hot Shoppes on Summit Avenue, and the Boar & Castle on West Market, which had already been around for more than a decade.

Most of the drive-ins went by the wayside when highways started being replaced by interstates and car culture gave way to video games. Sonic's still around, but unlike the old places, it's a national cookie-cutter chain rather than a local business, and somehow that's just not quite the same.

Military

The Army ORD closed for good, with more than 330,000 soldiers having passed through its gates. The Bessemer Improvement Company bought 433 acres of the property and nearly half the buildings, then designated the area for residential use.

1947

Baseball

The all-Black Goshen Red Wings baseball team became the Greensboro Red Wings. Several members of the Red Wings would go on to play for Negro National League teams, and one, first baseman Tom Alston, would become the first Black player on the St. Louis Cardinals roster in 1954.

Alston, a Greensboro native out of North Carolina A&T, stood an imposing 6 feet, 5 inches tall. He had his best season with San Diego of the Pacific Coast League — then almost a third major league — in 1953, where he hit .297 with 23 home runs and 101 runs batted in.

Suddenly, he was a hot commodity. The Padres traded him to St. Louis of the National League the following season, with the Cardinals paying $100,000 and sending four players to San Diego in the deal. It was a tidy profit for the San Diego club, which had purchased his contract from a Class-C ballclub in Porterville, California, for $100 just a year earlier.

The Cards had fielded a segregated team under Fred Saigh, who owned the ballclub from 1947 to 1953. But when Anheuser-Busch bought the team in '53, integration was on their to-do list. So they brought in longtime Negro League catcher Quincy Trouppe to find a good Black prospect, and the search led them to Alston, who hadn't played high school ball (Dudley High didn't have a team) but had started playing with organized teams during a stint in the Navy in 1944.

Alston was 27 years old by the time he had his breakthrough season with the Padres, but the team fudged his age as 22 to make him more attractive to major league teams who might want to buy his contract.

The subterfuge worked — accompanied by some high

praise from Padres manager Lefty O'Doul, the former two-time National League batting champion. O'Doul gushed that Alston was capable of hitting 50 homers in the majors.

The Cardinals held a big media event to introduce him at the Beverly Hills Hotel in Hollywood. But he never lived up to his billing as the next big thing.

When Alston hit just .246 with four homers and 34 RBI in 66 games for the Cards, the owners started to grumble that the Padres had cheated them. He played parts of the next three seasons with St. Louis, seeing limited action, before retiring.

During his time with the Cardinals, he started hearing voices in his head, which drove him to slit his wrists in a failed suicide attempt and later, after he'd left the team, to burn down the New Goshen Methodist Church. He later said the voices told him to do so because the congregation needed a new building.

Alston spent eight years in a psychiatric hospital before finally being discharged in 1967. He was inducted into the North Carolina A&T sports hall of fame five years later and died of prostate cancer in 1993.

Dining

A new S&W Cafeteria was built just east of the corner of Elm and Market.

S&W was part of a chain that started in Charlotte when Frank Odell Sherill and Fred Weber, two former mess sergeants during World War I, started serving cafeteria food in an Ivey's department store.

Their first restaurant, at

Greensboro's S&W is gone, but this one in Asheville still stands. *Author photo*

100 West Trade Street in Charlotte, was followed by others in places like Asheville, Atlanta, Chattanooga, Knoxville, Raleigh, and Roanoke.

And Greensboro.

S&W specialized in Southern cooking like country-style steak with pan gravy, whipped potatoes, and buttered mixed vegetables — a meal you could get for 75 cents in 1970 — turkey, or custard pie. In a letter to the *News & Record*, former patron Martha Sharpe recalled entering through a revolving door and enjoying organ music that was played inside.

Golf

The U.S. Women's Open came to Greensboro's Starmount Forest in just the tournament's second year. Betty Jameson of San Antonio won by six strokes, shooting 9 under par to set a course record and claim the $1,200 top prize. Her card included an eagle and seven birdies.

Sally Sessions of Michigan placed second after winning a playoff with fellow amateur Polly Riley.

Jameson would finish her career with 13 LPGA Tour wins, including three majors: the U.S. Women's Open at Starmount and two Women's Western Open titles a dozen years apart, in 1942 as an amateur and 1954.

Government

Fielding L. Fry became mayor; he would serve two years.

Weather

September was the wettest month on record in Greensboro, with 13.3 inches of rain falling during the month. More than half of that, 7.5 inches, fell on one day, September 24. That was a record for any single day in city history.

1948

Industry

A merger of Proximity Manufacturing and Revolution Mills created a new combined company called Cone Mills Manufacturing.

1949

Baseball

Luis Arroyo, a future major-leaguer and twice an All-Star, pitched a no-hitter for Greensboro and wound up with a 21-10 record on the mound, but the Patriots finished a game under .500.

Cinema

The 395-car North Drive-In opened on May 4 out on U.S. 29. It would get a new name, the Skyline, in 1962 when Jim Bellows — who'd purchased the South Drive-In a year earlier — bought the theater.

SKYLINE *U.S. 29 NORTH*
DRIVE-IN THEATRE New Reidsville Road Phone 272-8953

The Skyline, whose manager had an office and living quarters inside the screen, featured dusk-to-dawn movie marathons in the late sixties. One weekend special screened the Sean Connery James Bond movies in running order from *Dr. No* to *You Only Live Twice*.

The theater closed in 1980. ...

The Center Theatre opened on August 1 at 117 South Elm Street. The *Greensboro Daily News* reported that Mayor Ben Cone was on hand to sell the first ticket, and roses were handed out to women in attendance.

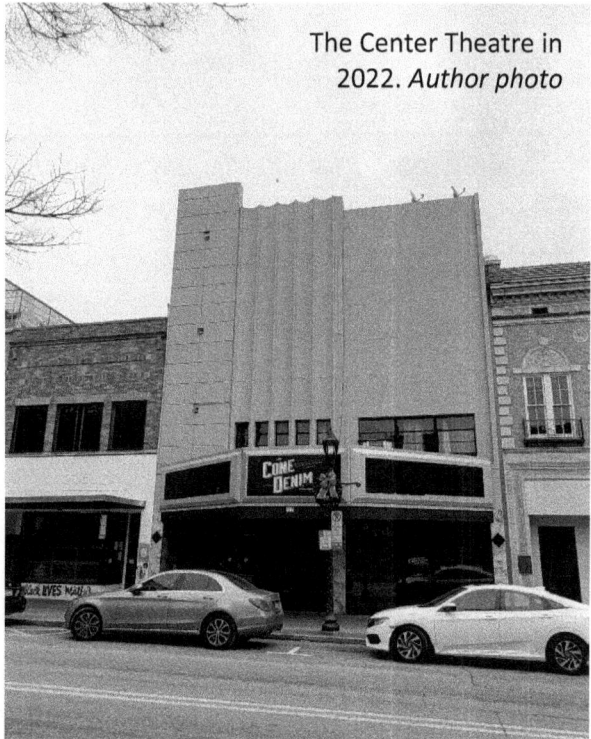

The Center Theatre in 2022. *Author photo*

It was a new beginning, but movies were hardly new to the location.

In fact, motion pictures in that space went all the way back to 1914, when the Piedmont Theatre opened there, hosting vaudeville shows along with silent movies. Just five years later, it was remodeled and got a new name: the Victory Theatre (not to be confused with the theater of the same name that opened in 1942 on Tate Street).

But that name just lasted a couple of years, giving way to the Imperial nameplate in 1921.

The Imperial was a grand movie house with 1,750 seats, but the Center took up just part of that space: There were 450 seats on the floor level and 310 more in a balcony with upper and lower sections.

The Center would operate until 1981, including a stint in the seventies when it showed martial arts and X-rated films.

Education

The Woman's College of the University of North Carolina was recognized as the largest college for women in the United States.

The Magnolia House in 2022. *Author photo*

Lodging

The Magnolia House, a hotel catering to Black travelers, opened at 442 Gorrell Street. It would be featured in six editions of Victor Hugo Green's *Negro Motorist Green Book*, a guide to inns, service stations, garages, restaurants, and other businesses that served Black motorists in the Jim Crow era. (African Americans often carried lunches packed in shoeboxes in case there was no *Green Book* eatery near where they were staying.)

During the years 1955 to 1961, the *Green Book* listed the Magnolia House — sometimes called the Magnolia Hotel and Magnolia Traveler's Motel — as one of five hotels in Greensboro that provided safe lodging for Black travelers.

The Magnolia House attracted a number of well-known

and accomplished African Americans during its heyday, including the likes of Jackie Robinson, Ray Charles, James Brown, Joe Tex, Ruth Brown, Satchel Paige, and Ike and Tina Turner.

As of 2021, the Magnolia House was one of just four *Green Book* sites in North Carolina still in operation.

The building that now houses the Elm Street Center was a modern Ellis-Stone Department Store when it opened in 1948. *Author photo*

Retail

Ellis-Stone, a local merchant, opened a new, modern department store on South Elm Street. The building was the work of a New York architectural firm called Vorhees, Walker, Foley, and Smith.

The firm had designed several buildings in New York City, including 1 Wall Street, the New York Telephone Co. headquarters, and the Barclay-Vesey building. One of the partners, Paul Walker, had even been named "architect of the century" by others in the field.

The building would be sold eight years later to Thalhimers, a chain that started in Richmond and expanded to include about two dozen branches at various times up to 1980. The former Ellis-Stone was the fourth and largest branch in the Thalhimers chain at 78,000 square feet.

Thalhimers also opened branches at the Friendly Center in 1958 and the Four Seasons Mall in 1975.

Government

Benjamin Cone, a Navy veteran and son of mill magnate Ceasar Cone, began a two-year term as mayor, while Juliette Dwiggins became the first woman to serve on the city council. She served two years before retiring.

Television

WFMY had been granted an FCC license to operate in Greensboro and was all set to introduce North Carolina to the new medium of television. It had signed a contract to affiliate with CBS-TV, and everything was set to go.

But then, it didn't.

Unfortunately, the station's main tower fell over before it could hit the airwaves, enabling Charlotte's WBTV to sign on first July 15, 1949. The announcement that aired that day was anything but epic: "Now we present a test pattern and tone for set adjustment."

WFMY followed later that year, debuting on September 22 as the nation's 76th television station. Both stations were owned by the Jefferson-Pilot Corporation. It made its first news broadcasts from a small building on Davie Street downtown.

Suburban Surge
1950–1959

Elm Street in the 1950s. *State Archives of North Carolina*

1950

Cinema

The Park Drive-In opened with room for 400 cars at 4421 Lawndale Drive. The screen was more than just a screen: It even had a five-room apartment inside the screen tower, facing the highway. Trees surrounded the property, making fencing unnecessary.

Plaza Manor played host to a number of Black luminaries. *Author photo*

Lodging

Plaza Manor Hotel, described in the *Greensboro Daily News* as "a new residence-hotel for Negroes," opened at 511 Martin Street.

The 22-room steam-heated concrete block structure was owned and operated by Donnie Edwards until his death in 1966. Guests who stopped there included Duke Ellington, Louis Armstrong, and the Harlem Globetrotters.

Milestones

Greensboro's population rose to 74,389 by the end of the 1940s, an increase of 25.4 percent from the start of the decade.

Retail

The Summit Shopping Center, Greensboro's first regional center, opened across from St. Leo's Hospital at Summit and Bessemer avenues, with an A&P as its anchor store. Also in 1950, the Lawndale Shopping Center on Lawndale Drive opened, anchored by Big Bear and Ralph's Food Palace.

The Summit in 2022. *Author photo*

Television

On September 30, Greensboro was treated to a televised broadcast from South Bend, Indiana, on WFMY: a college football game between North Carolina and powerhouse Notre Dame. Local viewers must have liked what they saw, at least in the third quarter when Carolina pulled even with the mighty Irish at 7-7.

UNC was no slouch: The Tar Heels came into the game ranked No. 20 by the Associated Press. But the Fighting Irish sat atop the rankings and were riding a 38-game unbeaten streak. North Carolina put that in jeopardy, but Notre Dame eked out a win on Bib Williams' 26-yard touchdown pass with less than 3 minutes to play.

The final score: 14-7.

The following week, Purdue toppled the Irish from their perch and ended their streak with a 28-14 upset.

1951

Government

Robert H. Frazier, a lawyer, began his two-year tenure as mayor. Meanwhile, William Hampton became the first Black member of the city council; he would be re-elected in 1953 and later serve on the city school board.

Industry

Cone Mills Manufacturing went public, with shares available for purchase on the New York Stock Exchange.

Retail

A Colonial market anchored the new Irving Park Plaza on Battleground Avenue.

Television

The first locally produced children's program in North Carolina aired on Greensboro's WFMY: *Six Gun Playhouse* (later rechristened *The Old Rebel Show*.

1952

Development

Joseph Koury founded the Koury Corporation. The company would go on to develop projects ranging from residential developments to hotels, golf courses, shopping centers, and industrial parks in the Piedmont Triad area.

Retail

Kroger opened its first store in Greensboro on May 20 at 1615 Garden Street. It would remain open for 21 years.

1953

Athletics

Representatives of seven schools met at midnight in the Sedgefield Inn to make what was then a radical decision: They banded together to leave the Southern Conference.

That athletic league had grown to a sprawling 23 members by 1932 before a number of schools withdrew to form the Southeastern Conference. But membership had become bloated again, growing to 17 members, by 1952. So seven of them left.

Duke, Maryland, Wake Forest, North Carolina State, North Carolina, Clemson, and South Carolina joined Virginia (which had played as an independent) to form the new Atlantic Coast Conference.

Dining

Walter Stamey opened a barbecue drive-in on High Point Road (now Gate City Boulevard), introducing Greensboro to Lexington-style barbecue.

He'd learned the technique from Sid Weaver and Jess Swicegood, who'd developed a technique of smoking pork shoulders rather than whole hogs, then adding a sauce that blended vinegar and pepper with ketchup.

Weaver and Swicegood were selling their barbecued pork

out of tents across from the courthouse. Stamey was still in high school in Lexington at the time. The year was 1927.

Lexington is a less than 40 miles southwest of Greensboro, but Stamey initially went in the opposite direction: He moved farther southwest, past Charlotte to Shelby, where he shared the technique with Red Bridges and Alston Bridges (not related), who opened restaurants of their own in 1946 and 1956.

Red Bridges Barbecue Lodge on Highway 74 and Alston Bridges Barbecue on Grover Street were both still going strong in 2022.

But Stamey left Shelby in 1938 and returned to Lexington, where he paid $300 to buy Swicegood's restaurant. He then opened a drive-in, a Snack Shop, and even had a franchise for ice-cream dispensers. It was in 1953 that he opened his Greensboro drive-in, which he passed along to his son Charles four years later.

Stamey's remains in business today, offering menu items like Brunswick stew, hushpuppies, slaw, and collard greens, along with chopped and sliced pork barbecue. ...

Libby Hill Seafood opened its doors at New Garden Road and U.S. Highway 220, founded by Luke and Elizabeth Conrad. The restaurant got its start in an old roadhouse that the sheriff had padlocked because it had played host to some questionable activities.

The restaurant — which initially served only fried seafood — later moved up the road and added steak to the menu, along with chicken.

It remained open as of 2022.

1954

Retail

Ralph's Food Palace on Lawndale Drive burned down after six years in business, but it wasn't the end of the road for the independent grocer. The store was rebuilt as just plain Ralph's, creating a fun atmosphere for shoppers with cartoon murals and aisle markers emblazoned with street names such as "Pickledilly Lane."

1955

Explosion

A crop duster pilot couldn't have been expecting what he saw in August during what was supposed to be a routine flight. All of a sudden, a quarter-mile away, the pilot saw flames and debris shooting skyward, up to his level, 1,000 feet in the air.

Something had exploded at the oil refinery off Winston Road.

The blast at the High Point Oil Company, a mile south of the airport, killed distillery plant operator Rufus Whitaker instantly. His body was found buried beneath a burning pile of twisted metal, oil-soaked clay, and other debris.

Whitaker's assistant, Carl Thompson, was left in extremely critical condition, and two other men were badly burned in the blast.

Government

R. Boyd Morris served a year as mayor, though he would resign in 1956.

Retail

Kroger opened its second Greensboro location, at 432 Bellemeade Street downtown, on June 28.

The 18,000-square-foot location had nine checkstands and a parcel pickup system. It was later demolished to make way for the current baseball stadium. ...

The city's second Big Bear market opened in Proximity Mill Village on Fourth Street. Two more stores would open in the sixties: an 18,000-square-foot store stocked with more than 5,000 items on March 2, 1964, and a store at the new Sedgefield Center High Point Road five years after that.

The former was next to a King's Department Store on West Market Street and featured a lounge where husbands and children could hang out while the lady of the house did her shopping. It was a different era. ...

Several local grocers, looking for a way to pay for advertising so they could compete with regional chains, joined forces to form a cooperative they dubbed Bi-Rite stores. Robert Butler, whose store in the Glenwood neighborhood had been open since 1936, adopted the new name for his market.

The fledgling chain would open new stores on Lawndale Drive in 1957 and High Point Road in 1959. Bi-Rite beat other chains into the southeast and eastern areas of the city before they were fully developed.

Bi-Rite would continue to grow in the 1960s, replacing established stores like Colonial and Piggly Wiggly in some cases, and opening new ones such as Butler's Bi-Rite on Battleground Avenue in September 1969. By the end of the sixties, there were 15 Bi-Rites in Greensboro.

But the chain would splinter after that, with some stores

in the cooperative, including Butler's locations, rebranding themselves as Bestway. By 1975, that new chain included eight stores, five of which were former Bi-Rites, but it would file for bankruptcy a decade later. A store operating under that name, however, still existed in 2022 at 2113 Walker Avenue.

By then, only one Bi-Rite remained: a Stokesdale store affiliated with Galaxy Foods.

The Bestway brand can still be found on Walker Avenue. *Author photo*

1956

Football

The Greensboro High School band performed at halftime of an NFL game between Washington and the Detroit Lions.

Golf

The clubhouse at Starmount Forest Golf Club burned down in May; a new one would open the following spring.

Government

J. Archie Cannon Jr. began a one-year stint as mayor of Greensboro.

Television

WFMY aired its first color telecast, spotlighting the state's Azalea Festival in Wilmington.

1957

Bowling

The 17th annual Southeastern Duckpin Tournament, described by the *Charlotte Observer* as the "Daddy" of all bowling events in the South, was held at the Greensboro Bowling Alleys.

Civil Rights

Before the Woolworth lunch counter in Greensboro became the site of sit-ins protesting racial segregation, a golf course was ground zero in the fight for racial equality.

Gillespie Park was an 18-hole course owned by the city and the county school board. But those owners had no interest in allowing African Americans to play there. In fact, when a group asked to do so in 1949, the owners responded by leasing the course to a private company.

The Gillespie Golf Club was a nonprofit group that charged membership and green fees. Under the club's official policy, only members were allowed on the course. But unofficially, any white golfer who could pay the green fee got to play.

A separate nine-hole course called Nacho Park was reserved for Black golfers.

The policy at Gillespie Park allowed the owners to keep

the course segregated by simply refusing African Americans membership, and it remained in place until it was challenged by Greensboro dentist George Simkins Jr., leader of the local NAACP branch.

When Simkins and five other African Americans tried to play there, they were convicted of trespassing and sentenced to 30 days of road labor. The sentences were ultimately commuted as a discrimination lawsuit brought by Simkins against the city made its way through federal court.

On March 20, the court ruled that the city and the school board could not avoid offering equal facilities to Black golfers by leasing the course to a private group:

"...the right of citizens to use public property without discrimination on the ground of race may not be abridged by the mere leasing of the property," the court stated. But then, it gave the owners an escape hatch: "The city may, however, under the terms of the order, part with ownership of the property by bona fide sale."

That's exactly what the city did. Instead of integrating Gillespie Park, it closed both that course and the Nacho Park course. Even so, the decision was a milestone, going beyond *Brown v. Board of Education of Topeka* in overturning segregation for entities other than public schools.

Community

Greensboro annexed the town of Hamilton Lakes, the community of Bessemer, Pomona Mill village, and the Hamtown neighborhood. ...

The Greensboro Junior Museum opened in a 38-by-80-foot, $28,000 nature center at Country Park. Initially a Junior League project, it would be taken over by the city three years later. It would later become the Natural Science Center of Greensboro and, finally, the Greensboro Science Center.

Education

The Negro Agricultural and Technical College of North Carolina changed its name to Agricultural and Technical College of North Carolina. The first white student, Rodney Jaye Miller of Greensboro, gained admission.

Government

George H. Roach served as mayor from 1957 until 1961.

Macy's at the Friendly Center in 2022. *Author photo*

Retail

Friendly Center opened as a relatively modest (compared to today) outdoor center consisting of two blocks, each with a dozen stores.

Still, it was a big deal for the time: Its 1,300 parking spaces were all filled on opening day, when 25,000 shoppers turned out to visit stores like Friendly Toy & Hobby, Carolina Camera center, Willis Book & Stationery, Mason's Florist, and Jay's Deli. Laurie's Sportswear was the first fashion retailer to leave downtown for the suburbs.

Major retail tenants included Belk (which had a store downtown), Woolworth, Eckerd Drugs, and Colonial Stores — a supermarket

Sign at entrance to Friendly Center. *Author photo*

chain later absorbed by Big Star; still later, most of the Big Stars became Harris Teeter locations. Belk's 24,000-square-foot store featured a mural that rose 12 feet high and spanned 70 feet on the mezzanine, depicting local landmarks.

As of 2019, Belk and Jay's Deli were the only original tenants remaining in the center, which had grown to include six anchor tenants and encompass more than 1.23 million square feet of retail space. ...

Winn-Dixie anchored the new Florida Street Shopping Center at Freeman Mill Road. ...

Colonial Stores opened a new 16,500-square-foot market on High Point Road. It would add another of similar size on Asheboro Street in 1959, bringing the chain to five stores in the city by the end of the decade.

1958

Development

Joseph Koury started buying land south of downtown, which he planned to use for housing and retail development. It would become the site of the Four Seasons Towne Center mall.

Retail

Southside Shopping Center on Asheboro Street opened. Colonial served as its anchor store. ...

A New York-based chain called Clark's opened a store September 11 in an old tobacco warehouse on Burlington Road. The location was big at 120,000 square feet, and it needed to be: A novel concept at the time, the store fused a discount department store with a supermarket under a single roof.

Clark's, one of the first large stores to stay open on Sundays, also opened in Charlotte and Winston-Salem about this time.

The chain was purchased by a Cleveland company and rebranded as Cook's around 1970, and the first Greensboro store stayed open until 1977.

1959

Community

The $4.5 million Greensboro Coliseum Complex, first conceived 15 years earlier, was completed. The complex included the Coliseum itself, with a seating capacity of 7,100, along with the War Memorial Auditorium, Town Hall Auditorium, and Blue Room.

Holiday on Ice, the first event ever held at the complex, began a six-show run on October 29 and had drawn 37,447 spectators by the time it ended its engagement November 3.

Fast Food

A couple of World War II veterans opened the first McDonald's in North Carolina opened on 1101 Summit Avenue at Bessemer on September 30. The chain had fewer than 500 stores at the time, and hamburgers sold for 15 cents.

McDonald's is in a newer building but the same location as the original on Summit Avenue. *Author photo*

Ice Hockey

The Troy Bruins had a new league and a new home: in Greensboro. The Bruins, who had played the previous season in the International Hockey League, switched to the Eastern Hockey League and became the Greensboro Generals.

Carson Bain, who would serve as Greensboro's mayor from 1967 to 1969, led a team of investors that owned the team.

The Generals opened their inaugural season October 24 with a 4-3 win on the road against the Clinton Comets. Their first home game, a 4-1 victory over the Washington Presidents on November 11, drew a crowd of 3,014 to the brand-new Greensboro Coliseum.

Retail

A Big Bear market highlighted the new Northeast Shopping Center at Bessemer and Summit avenues. The 17,200-square-foot store, which opened November 10 and featured one of the chain's distinctive deli-kitchens, replaced the one that had opened four years earlier on Fourth Street.

It was advertised as the "most completely equipped and stocked store in North Carolina."

Friendly Center added six new spaces, including Ellis-Stone, which would later become Thalhimers. A post office and an ABC Store also made their debut.

A satellite view shows Greensboro Coliseum in 2007. *USGS-NASA*

It Happened at Woolworth's
1960–1969

1960

Woolworth in Greensboro was the site of the first lunch counter sit-in protesting segregation. *Author photo*

Bowling

Fair Lanes Friendly Bowlarama opened. A fire on the weekend of its first anniversary a year later would cause extensive damage, but the lanes were not affected.

Civil rights

It all started in Greensboro, at what was then an American institution: the Woolworth's lunch counter.

Back in the day, F.W. Woolworth was everywhere. Founded in 1879, it had 120 five-and-dime stores a quarter-century later. Its New York headquarters, built in 1913, was the world's tallest building until the Empire State Building surpassed it. The company had 2,250 outlets by the time the of the stock market crash in '29, and its discount format enabled it to survive the Depression.

Woolworth had cheap food, too. You didn't just shop there, you could grab a bite to eat at the store's lunch counter, which was as iconic as the chain itself. Some people who didn't shop at Woolworth's even went there *just* to have lunch.

F.W. Woolworth Co.

PLAIN or TOASTED SANDWICHES	
BACON and TOMATO 50c	
Toasted Three Decker Sandwich	
BAKED HAM and CHEESE 60c	
Toasted Three Decker Sandwich	HAM SALAD Sandwich............30c
CHICKEN SALAD 65c	EGG SALAD Sandwich............30c
Toasted Three Decker Sandwich	
HAM SALAD and EGG SALAD 50c	AMERICAN CHEESE Sandwich......30c
Toasted Three Decker Sandwich	
Above available on two slices of bread on request.	PRESSED HAM Sandwich.........30c

FOR A REAL TREAT!
TRY OUR SUPER DE LUXE HAM SANDWICH—BAKED HAM SLICED VERY THIN AND STACKED HIGH ON PLAIN BREAD, TOAST OR HARD ROLL
40¢ YOU WILL LIKE IT! 40¢

Fountain Features

DE LUXE
TULIP SUNDAE 25c
2 Dippers of Ice Cream covered with Crushed Fruit or Fresh Fruits in Season

CHOICE OF
STRAWBERRY, PINEAPPLE, CHERRY, CHOCOLATE OR HOT FUDGE
Topped with Whipped Topping Roasted Nuts and Cherry King

SUPER JUMBO
BANANA SPLIT 39c
½ Banana covered with 3 Dippers of Ice Cream and Crushed Fruits or Fresh Fruits in Season

CHOICE OF
STRAWBERRY, PINEAPPLE, CHERRY, CHOCOLATE OR HOT FUDGE
Topped with Whipped Topping and Roasted Nuts

EXTRA RICH
ICE CREAM SODA 25c
POPULAR FLAVORS
Made with 2 Dippers of Ice Cream Crushed Fruit or Fresh Fruits in Season

MALTED MILK 25c
Popular FLAVORS   Made with 2 Dippers of Ice Cream
MILK SHAKE 25c
Popular FLAVORS   Made with 2 Dippers of Ice Cream
BANANA SPLIT Regular.......................25c
Popular FLAVORS   Made with 3 Dippers of Ice Cream
FRESH ORANGE JUICE......... Regular 20c Large 30c
Freshly Squeezed to Order

HOT NESTLE'S WITH WHIPPED TOPPING.....15c
AND WAFERS

DRINK Coca-Cola
KING SIZE 10¢

APPLE PIE ....Per Cut 15c
10c Additional with Ice Cream
Home Style Desserts LAYER CAKE ....Per Cut 15c
10c Additional with Ice Cream

WOOLWORTH COFFEE — ALWAYS GOOD

HAVE A COKE   Coca-Cola   GOES GOOD WITH FOOD
NO. 345A REV. 9-60

In the 1950s, you could order a ham-and-egg-salad sandwich or a BLT minus the lettuce for 50 cents. Baked ham and cheese cost a little more at 60 cents, and chicken salad was the menu's high-end item, checking in at 65 cents. Each of those sandwiches was a triple decker, but if you were really on a budget, you could have one of four other sandwiches, plain or toasted, for 30 cents each.

But a lot of folks went to the lunch counter for the soda fountain (featuring Coca-Cola) and ice cream. Popular items included an ice cream soda, milkshake, or regular banana split for a quarter, and the "super jumbo" banana split for 39 cents. Those who preferred a different kind of dessert could get a slice of layer cake or apple pie for 15 cents.

The heyday of the Woolworth lunch counter is packed with fond memories for a lot of people in Greensboro and elsewhere... all of them white. During the 1950s, Black patrons weren't allowed to stop in for a milkshake or a grilled cheese sandwich. They couldn't even sit at the lunch counter, let alone eat there. It was considered off limits, reserved strictly for white customers.

So were other lunch counters at five-and-dimes across the South.

But four black freshmen at North Carolina A&T — Ezell A. Blair Jr., Franklin E. McCain, Joseph A. McNeil and David L. Richmond — were determined to change all that. On February 1, 1960, they sat down at the Woolworth counter on Elm Street and ordered a cup of coffee. Predictably, they were refused service and told to leave, but they stood (or sat) firm, staying in their seats until closing time.

Older Blacks had been enduring the abuses of segregation for decades, but the younger generation wasn't having it.

"I don't like having to go to a separate section of a public place," the 17-year-old Blair said in an interview with the Associated Press. "Older Negroes have always put up with that because they were afraid of losing their jobs. As college students, we have no jobs to lose."

That first sit-in wasn't a one-off protest.

The day after it occurred, more students showed up at Woolworth's. By the third day 60 people were there, and five times that many showed up on the fourth. And that was just the beginning: The movement expanded up the street to the Kress five-and-dime, which had its own segregated lunch counter. Word spread, and so did the protests, with sit-ins being staged in Winston-Salem, Durham, Raleigh, Charlotte and across the South. Like wildfire, new protests flared in Baton Rouge, Louisiana; Charleston, South Carolina; Lexington, Kentucky; Nashville; Richmond, Virginia, and elsewhere.

But the segregationists were just as determined.

More than 1,000 demonstrators had been arrested by the end of April. But still, the segregationists held firm. When city officials suggested a compromise that would have allowed Blacks to sit at a reserved section of the lunch counter, managers at the Greensboro Kress and Woolworth stores rejected it out of hand.

It wasn't until the protests started taking a financial toll that Woolworth relented: By the time it integrated its lunch counter, Woolworth had lost an estimated $200,000. Other Woolworths ended their segregated lunch counters, too, as did the Kresge and W.T. Grant stores in Norfolk and Portsmouth, Virginia. But change didn't happen all at once, as some lunch counters in the South continued to bar people to people of color for as long as five years.

Eventually, the Greensboro Woolworth store closed, but the sign remains, and the site pays tribute to the protest that launched a movement: The lunch counter's still there, and the former store is now the site of the International Civil Rights Center and Museum.

Entertainment

Ringling Bros. and Barnum & Bailey Circus began a 50-year run of annual shows at the Greensboro Coliseum. The circus would draw nearly 3.5 million spectators to 500 performances in those 50 years.

Fast Food

Wilber Hardee was running a restaurant called the Silo in Greenville when he got wind of a new place that had just opened up in Greensboro called McDonald's. He heard it was doing a booming business, so Hardee decided to check it out.

Sure enough, they were raking in $168 an hour selling 15-cent burgers.

Hardee was impressed enough to snap a photo of the place and start making plans to open a restaurant along the same lines. He thought he could do it better. So contacted a builder to put up a smaller version of the McDonald's he'd photographed, then rent it to him.

The building on 14th Street near East Carolina University featured the same red and white tiles he'd seen at McDonald's, two service windows for ordering and pickup. The first Greensboro Hardee's opened on September 3, less than a year after McDonald's arrived in town.

He added char-grills to get a leg up on McDonald's, but the prices were similar: 15 cents bought you a hamburger, cheeseburgers were 20 cents, and you could also get fries, shakes, soft drinks, and fried apple pies.

The formula was an instant success, and Hardee made $9,500 in profits during just his first month in business. He opened a second location in Rocky Mount with two partners, but the relationship soured and they wound up owning the business, even though it kept Hardee's name.

Lodging

By 1960, the General Greene Motel was operating on U.S. Highway 70 and 29 between Greensboro and High Point, offering (according to a postcard) "new and modern sound-proof rooms, individually controlled heat and air conditioning, room T.V., room phones, combination tub and shower, and wall-to-wall carpet."

AAA described it as a "very pleasant, nicely furnished, one- and two-story motel with 59 rooms." It even had a swimming pool with a diving board.

And for breakfast, dinner, or a cup of coffee you could head next door to Howard Johnson's Restaurant. Howard Johnson's was famous for its 28 flavors of ice cream and fried clam strips, which the chain called "tendersweet clams." But you could also get a variety of sandwiches with potato chips, broiled chicken, steak, ham and eggs, and for dessert, a slice of fudge cake, Boston cream pie, or apple pie.

Milestones

Another big decade of growth (60.7 percent) saw Greensboro surge into six figures, population-wise, at 119,574, by 1960. The city was now the 100th-biggest in the United States and second-largest in North Carolina, behind Charlotte.

Politics

Vice President Richard Nixon got a staph infection after bumping his knee on a car door during a campaign stop in Greensboro. It was just 40 days before his crucial first presidential debate with John F. Kennedy.

Nixon, the Republican nominee, ended up in the hospital for 12 days and had surgery on the knee, losing 20 pounds in the process.

Then, when he arrived for the televised debate —

John F. Kennedy and Richard Nixon before their first debate.

the first of its kind — in Chicago, he hit the knee on a car door again. Already feverish the night before, he appeared on camera looking pale and sweaty. The debate was widely considered a turning point in the race, which Nixon lost by just 0.2 percent of the total votes cast.

He later claimed the infection sustained in Greensboro cost him the election.

1961

Fast Food

A new Biff-Burger outlet opened on May 3 at 1040 West Lee Street (now Gate City Boulevard).

The chain, founded in 1956 in Clearwater, Florida, had restaurants stretching all the way north to Toronto at its peak. "Biff" stood for "Best in fast food," and cooked its burgers using what it called a roto-broiled system: The beef patties were cooked on the upper level of a double-deck rotisserie, and the juices would drip down to the lower rack, onto the buns.

Beef Burger, formerly Biff-Burger, on Gate City Boulevard, with its mascot. *Author photo*

Like many burger chains that opened at the time, it offered hamburgers for 15 cents each.

Ralph Havis started working at the Greensboro location on Lee Street the year it opened (it was actually one of three Biff-Burgers in town) and kept working there for the next 10 years. He even met his wife when she showed up at the window to order a fish sandwich one day.

Then, in 1971, when the franchise owner decided he'd had enough of running the business, he offered Havis the franchise on interest-free financing. He paid off the $60,000 purchase price over five years in monthly installments of $1,000.

A decade later, though, the Biff-Burger chain went out of business, so Havis — not wanting to risk using a company name he might not be entitled to — rebranded the outlet as Beef Burger (although longtime customers kept using the original name).

Beef Burger closed in 2021. *Author photo*

Over the years, Havis expanded the originally basic menu from 10 or 15 items to more than 100, including 30 flavors of milkshake. You could order everything from corn nuggets to chicken livers, from a "Bologna Supreme" to a vegetarian box dinner, from a "Flounderwich" to fried okra.

It was the last remaining Biff-Burger still operating as of 2021 when it finally closed for good in May. A sign taped to the door read: "Ralph appreciates all the thoughts and prayers from customers and friends. We humbly thank you all for years of service. Thank you, Greensboro!"

Havis had been hospitalized that same month. He passed away at the age of 78 in July.

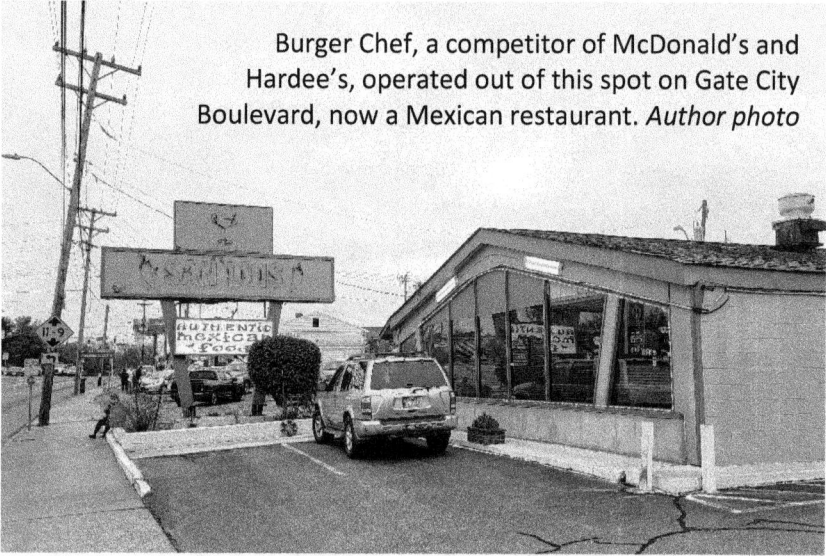

Burger Chef, a competitor of McDonald's and Hardee's, operated out of this spot on Gate City Boulevard, now a Mexican restaurant. *Author photo*

Golf

Charlie Sifford became the first Black golfer to play a major PGA tournament in the Deep South, but he wasn't about to settle for just making an appearance. He opened the Greater Greensboro Open with a 3-under-par 68 to take a one-stroke lead into the second round.

Sifford, a native of Charlotte, wasn't new to the game. He'd won the National Negro Open six times (including a string from 1952 to 1956) and was 38 years old by the time he became the first Black player to join the PGA Tour in 1961.

He went on to win two official tour events, but Greensboro wasn't one of them, as he faded with a final-round 75. That was still good enough for a share of fourth place and a $1,300 paycheck. Mike Souchak won the tournament going away, putting seven strokes between himself and the field as he played every round under par.

Sifford's tour victories came at the Greater Hartford Open in 1967 and the Los Angeles Open in 1969. He also won the PGA Seniors' Championship, for golfers over 50, in 1975. He was the first Black player inducted into the World Golf Hall of Fame, and he received the Presidential Medal of Freedom in 2014. Tiger Woods would name his son Charlie for Sifford.

Government

David Schenck took over as mayor; he would serve until 1965.

Retail

A $350,000 A&P supermarket, complete with a full-service meat department, anchored the brand-new Golden Gate Shopping Center, which opened March 16 next to the upscale Irving Park Neighborhood.

A&P continued expanding in Greensboro throughout the decade, opening a 15,000-square-foot store on Battleground Avenue in 1963 that included a "magic carpet door" that opened and closed automatically.

Two other new branches, in Coliseum Center on West Florida Street and Spring Valley Shopping Center on South Ashe Street (Randleman Road) followed in 1966, and by the end of the decade, the chain had doubled its footprint in Greensboro from five to 10 stores.

1962

Community

Greensboro had grown to 50 square miles, according to the City Directory.

It had 29 parks, 206 churches, and 36 public schools. There

were more than 36,000 registered automobiles and more than 441 miles of paved roads to drive them on.

Two daily and three weekly newspapers were available. If you preferred electronic media, you could turn your radio dial to one of five stations or choose between two television channels: WFMY and WUMC, both 100,000 watts strong.

1963

Education

The Woman's College of the University of North Carolina was a women's college no more. Upon admitting men for the first time, it needed a new name, and it got one: University of North Carolina at Greensboro.

Ice Hockey

After pacing the Southern Division for a third consecutive year, the Greensboro Generals finally went all the way.

The Generals, winners of 16 in a row at one point, outscored their opponents 71-31 in one 13-game stretch during the run. They finished the season tied with the Northern Division champion Clinton Comets for the most points in the league (82) and won more games than any other team (40).

Gary Sharp and Bob Boucher scored 60 goals apiece during the regular season, with Don Davidson supplying a team-leading 81 assists. Sharp added 61 assists to finish with 121 points, a club record.

But the regular season was just the beginning: Since eight of the league's nine teams qualified for the playoffs, the Generals had to survive three rounds of postseason play to claim the championship. The first round was easy, as they dispatched last-place Nashville in three straight games.

It got harder after that.

The Generals were pushed to the limit in the semifinals before turning back the Charlotte Checkers in five games to earn a spot in the best-of-seven finals against Clinton. There, they prevailed in six games, including a double-overtime contest that lasted 96 minutes, with Pat Kelly scoring the winning goal.

1964

Education

Jesse Jackson, civil rights activist and future presidential candidate, graduated from North Carolina A&T.

The Barn Dinner Theatre on Stage Coach Trail is the nation's oldest continuously operating dinner theater.
Author photo

Theater

The Barn Theatre — with a hydraulic "Magic Stage" that descended from the ceiling before each act — opened at 120

Stage Coach Trail; as of 2022, it was the nation's oldest continuously operated dinner theater.

The Barn wasn't the first of its kind. In fact, it was the second in a chain of regional theaters dedicated to bringing big-city shows to smaller southern cities like Greensboro. The first one opened in 1961 in Roanoke, and the chain eventually grew to 27 in North Carolina, Virginia, Tennessee, Georgia, Louisiana, New York, and Texas.

Legend has it that future Oscar-winner Robert De Niro was acting there in 1967 when he was fired during the middle of a production called *Tchin-Tchin* (billed as an adult comedy with a New York cast) for refusing to wait tables.

As it happens, though, a legend may be all it is.

De Niro did, in fact, perform at the Barn. He played the leading role of construction worker Ceasario Grimaldi, taking over from Anthony Quinn, who'd been in the Broadway production. De Niro had just two film appearances under his belt at that point, and he wasn't paid much for his engagement at the Barn: $35 a week plus $3 a week in expenses and a place to stay at the theater.

But rather than being fired, De Niro said he enjoyed the arrangements, which indeed called for the actors to serve dessert to the guests before the start of the show.

1965

Government

W.L. Trotter Jr. began a two-year term as mayor.

Journalism

Norfolk-based Landmark Communications bought the *Greensboro Daily News* and the *Greensboro Record*.

The Daily News Building was later converted to serve as a portion of the Cultural Center. *Author photo*

1966

Baseball

Satchel Paige, the ageless future Hall of Famer, pitched two innings for Peninsula, yielding two runs on four hits in two innings of a 4-2 loss to Greensboro.

Community

Growth in Greensboro led to a major expansion at Courthouse Square. The historic courthouse, completed in 1920, was now just part of a larger overall complex: a $13 million Government Center, complete with a new underground parking garage.

The architecture of the new buildings, however, stood in stark contrast to that of the old courthouse. They were built in a blocky Brutalist style which had become popular in the mid-1950s and remained so in the '60s.

The term "Brutalism" stems from the French *béton brut*, meaning "raw concrete." About as far from the intricate stonework of classical styles as you can get, the buildings look plain and heavy, often with recessed windows.

Courthouse Square expansion. *Author photo*

Other examples of the style can be seen in the 10-story Walter Jackson Library at UNC-Greensboro, built in 1972, the 10-story First Union National Bank building at 122 North Elm, completed a year earlier, and the Federal Home Loan Bank of Greensboro at 444 North Elm, built in 1970.

The Federal Home Loan Bank of Greensboro. *Author photo*

Weather

The most snow in a single month for Greensboro, 22.9 inches, fell in January.

1967

Basketball

The Greensboro Coliseum played host to its first ACC Men's Basketball Tournament, with North Carolina defeating Duke 82-73 for the title.

Dining

If you liked pancakes, you had new place to go for breakfast: Uncle John's Pancake House.

Uncle John's was kind of like International House of Pancakes: It had a lot of different (and sometimes weird-sounding) menu items: African banana Pancakes, ginger bread pancakes, buckwheat Pancakes, Iowa corn pancakes, and so forth.

If you didn't like pancakes, you could always order French toast, waffles, or other breakfast favorites like bacon, ham, or sausage and eggs.

Uncle John's was a national chain that had something like 50 restaurants, mostly in the Sun Belt. You could find an Uncle John's in places like Fresno, Bakersfield, Las Vegas, Charlotte, and Houston. And now there was one in Greensboro, too. But it didn't stay for long.

Slater "Tex" Moore and his wife, Shirley, came to Greensboro from an Uncle John's in Lansing, Michigan, to help open the new restaurant. They took over the Greensboro franchise in 1970 and bought it outright two years later, changing the name to (fittingly) Tex & Shirley's.

The couple retired in 1989 and sold the restaurant to longtime manager Bart Ortiz, who'd first met them back at the Lansing restaurant when he was 16 years old, working as a dishwasher back in 1966.

The restaurant stayed open at 708 Pembroke Road until 2017, when it lost its lease and moved to 1617 West Friendly Avenue. Tex Moore, who'd moved back to his home state of Texas after selling the restaurant to Ortiz, returned to North Carolina in 2006 and opened another Tex & Shirley's in High Point. He passed away two years later at the age of 86, but that restaurant, like the original was still open in 2022.

Some of the menu items at the first Tex & Shirley's — like Manhattan pancakes, Swedish pancakes, dollar pancakes, and "Three Little Pigs in a Blanket" — date back to the Uncle John's days.

Government

Carson Bain kicked off a two-year term as mayor.

Retail

Another expansion at Friendly Center brought in several new stores, including the Gate City Pharmacy, K&W Cafeteria, Harvey West Music, and Cass Jewelers. A store called Potpourri epitomized the era, selling incense, blacklight posters, mood rings, and love beads.

1968

Cinema

A twin movie house called Janus Theatre opened in December at 1416 Northwood Street, showing the Beatles' animated *Yellow Submarine* and *Elvira Madigan*, a Swedish film about a Danish circus performer.

Expansions made it a four-screen theater in 1970 and a seven-screen venue in 1975, with an eighth screen being added by 1981. It eventually closed in 2000 and was torn down to be replaced by luxury condominiums and specialty shops.

Janus Theatre opened as a twin-screen cinema and then went through a series of expansions before closing in 2000. *Filmmaker1971, Creative Commons 2.0, cinematreasures*

Retail

Plans were announced for a new regional shopping center on Randleman Road to be called Greenbriar Mall. Woolco (Woolworth's foray into the discount store market) and Kroger had been signed up as anchors, and construction started on the center, but the project was never completed.

1969

Basketball

The Houston Mavericks had been a failure no matter how you look at it. The team finished dead last in the American Basketball Association's Western Division with a record of

23-55, but that would have been considered a success compared to their woeful attendance.

Houston was the sixth-largest city in the U.S. by 1970, but you wouldn't have known it if you'd seen the crowds in the Sam Houston Coliseum. A game there in December drew just 246 fans, and their final game, on April 2, drew just 89 people.

The news came out in January that, to no one's surprise, the team had been purchased. But the league tried to keep it a secret that the Mavericks would be moving, in order to maintain what little interest remained in Houston.

A headline in the *Statesville Record & Landmark* on January 3 revealed that the team had been sold for $650,000, but that the new owners would remain anonymous for about two weeks. It only took two days for the news to leak that a group called Southern Sports Corporation, headed by former congressman Jim Gardner, had purchased the team and planned to move it to North Carolina.

Gardner, a former chairman of the state Republican Party, would later serve as lieutenant governor from 1989 to 1993.

The Cougars, as they were christened, announced plans to split their games among three North Carolina metro areas, playing most often in Greensboro because the Greensboro Coliseum was the state's largest indoor facility. Other home games were set for Charlotte and Raleigh, making the team a "regional" franchise befitting its name. (No games, however, were set for South Carolina.) It was a formula that would be adopted a year later by the league's Virginia Squires.

Gardner immediately cut most of the team's ties with its Houston past, announcing he wouldn't be retaining coach Jim Weaver and adding: "As a matter of fact, we'll probably retain only three or four players off the current team. We have a massive rebuilding job to do."

The team hired Bones McKinney as its new coach and built a roster that included several players with North Carolina ties. Bill Bunting, Larry Miller, and Doug Moe were all UNC products; Gene Littles came from High Point University, and Bob Verga was a former star at Duke.

Verga had actually played with Houston the previous year, when he'd averaged 24.7 points as one of the few bright spots for the Mavs. With Carolina, he upped his game even further, averaging 27.5 a game and earning the only All-Star nod of his career.

Verga, Moe, and Littles each finished the season with more than 1,000 points as the Cougars posted a 42-42 record, good for third place in the Eastern Division and a major improvement on the Mavericks' mark the previous year. They even made the playoffs, although they were quickly dispatched by the Indiana Pacers in a four-game sweep.

Greensboro supported the team better than either of the other two state venues it called home, but wherever they played in North Carolina, far more fans turned out than had greeted the team in Houston. Average attendance that first season was 6,051.

Civil Rights

Gunshots rang out at North Carolina A&T after police used tear gas to disperse a crowd of student protesters at James B. Dudley High School on the evening of May 21.

When the shooting stopped, student Willie James Grimes — a bystander not involved in the protest — was dead. He'd been hit in the back of the head by a small-caliber bullet in Scott Hall dormitory on campus. No one ever found out who fired the shot that killed him.

Police were sent to Page High School after classes were

interrupted: Students there were upset that no African Americans had been elected to the cheerleading squad. But order was restored quickly there, and classes soon resumed.

It was a different story at Dudley High, where the tension had begun. Discontent had been brewing on campus there for some time, with officials placing restrictions on what students could wear and enforcing a closed-campus policy during lunch.

There Black students had begun protesting the school's refusal to allow Charles Barnes, an honors student who was Black, to run for student body president. Their rationale: He was a member of a club officials there didn't like that was linked with the Black Power movement. In order to run for office, a student had to be certified by a student-faculty committee — which had declined to do so in Barnes' case.

Barnes ran as a write-in candidate anyway and won in a landslide: His total of 600 votes was three times that of his nearest rival. But school officials refused to recognize his victory, and students at A&T rallied to support him May 2, engaging school officials in talks that went nowhere.

The administration wouldn't budge.

Tensions continued to build until May 19, when police arrested nine student protesters for alleged misconduct. That only fueled further protests, and police were called to the school again when a school official claimed to have seen a weapon on one of the students on Wednesday, May 21.

That same day, a judge issued a restraining order against 40 people — including Barnes and A&T student body president Vincent McCullough — prohibiting them from entering the Dudley campus or suggesting that students take skip classes there as part of a boycott.

As the protest grew, a school official tried to break it up, but students started throwing rocks at the school windows, and police deployed tear gas against them. The chaos violence spilled out of the school grounds as students fled into the neighborhood, pursued by police who fired more tear gas — so that some bystanders and area residents were overcome.

They retaliated by throwing rocks at the police and patrol cars.

Barely a mile away at North Carolina A&T, a carload of white students fired shots onto the campus, and some armed students fired back. Sniper fire was reported from one of the dorms, and police began firing, as well, with 150 National Guard members being dispatched to the scene by Governor Bob Scott.

Shots could be heard into the early morning of May 22, and Mayor Jack Elam responded by instituting a nighttime curfew and declaring a state of emergency.

The National Guard's numbers swelled to 600, and they used gunfire and tear gas to rout dozens of students from buildings at A&T, where classes at the university were suspended indefinitely. A tank and armored personnel carriers rolled onto campus, while an airplane dropped smoke canisters, and a helicopter released nausea gas.

One reporter called it "the most massive armed assault ever made against an American university."

The guardsmen ransacked Scott Hall, reported source of the sniping, smashing in doors before breaking up furniture and student property as they searched for weapons. Only two weapons were found.

"It looked like war," a UPI photojournalist said.

Three hundred students were hauled from various buildings, taken into custody, and sent to state prisons, where they were fingerprinted and kept for the remainder of the day.

One guardsman was reportedly shot early Friday morning,

May 23, with five police officers and a student also injured.

And then it was over.

The violence had ended by May 24, and the National Guard went home. The curfew was ended. A North Carolina State Advisory Committee told the U.S. Commission on Human Rights that Dudley High's policies were unjust and had been designed to quell dissent. It was, the committee wrote, "a sad commentary that the only group in the community who would take the Dudley students seriously were the students at A&T State University.

Two-thousand people attended Willie Grimes' funeral, and a memorial marker was erected to him on campus.

Government

H.J. "Jack" Elam III was elected to a two-year term as mayor.

Music

"Get Back" by the Beatles was at the top of the chart for the WCOG 1320 All-American Survey on May 12, followed by "Hair" from the Cowsills in the No. 2 position and "Aquarius/Let the Sunshine In" by the 5th Dimension.

Retail

A new Zayre department store opened on High Point Road at Holden Road, with a Big Star market owned by the Colonial chain opening next door.

Zayre, a discount chain founded in 1956 in Massachusetts, eventually encompassed 1,187 stores in 43 states and Washington, D.C. By 1990, the Zayre chain had ceased to exist, but a spinoff store founded in 1977 has continued to thrive: T.J. Maxx. As of 2022, that store had locations on Battleground

Avenue and Wendover Avenue in Greensboro.

The Zayre store, meanwhile, was taken over by Winn-Dixie in 1994.

Hardwood Heights

1970-1979

The Greensboro Coliseum was home to the Carolina Cougars pro basketball team and hosted an NCAA Tournament Final Four in the 1970s. *Author photo*

1970

Basketball

The Carolina Cougars started the season with eight straight losses and suffered an 11-game losing streak near the end of the 1970-71 season, sliding to a 34-50 overall record. They finished sixth in the Eastern Division despite a strong season from Joe Caldwell, who averaged 23.3 points a game.

Cinema

The Circle Drive-In opened March 4 with room for 300 cars at 305 Robbins Street. The grand opening featured Don Knotts in *The Shakiest Gun in the West* in a double bill with Phyllis Diller's *Did You Hear the One About the Traveling Saleslady?*

The Circle would remain open through 1983. ...

The new indoor theater on High Point Road had quite a name: the Trans-Lux In-Flight Cinema. It shifted course in 1976, remaking itself as an adult theater known as Cinema Blue (and, later, Royal Cine, which also featured live stage shows).

Lodging

A Holiday Inn opened on land Joseph Koury had purchased 12 years earlier.

Milestones

Greensboro was the nation's 94th-largest city. Its population had risen 20.5 percent to 144,076 during the' 60s.

Music

The Jackson 5 played a July 10 date at the Coliseum before 14,490 fans.

1971

Basketball

The East All-Stars defeated the West 126-122 before 14,407 fans in the ABA All-Star Game on January 23 at the Greensboro Coliseum. Joe Caldwell of the hometown Carolina Cougars scored 21 points and grabbed eight rebounds in a losing effort for the East.

The Cougars, however, posted another losing record during their third season in Carolina. They finished at 35-49, fifth in the Eastern Division.

Government

Jim Melvin was elected to the first of five consecutive terms as mayor; he would serve through 1981.

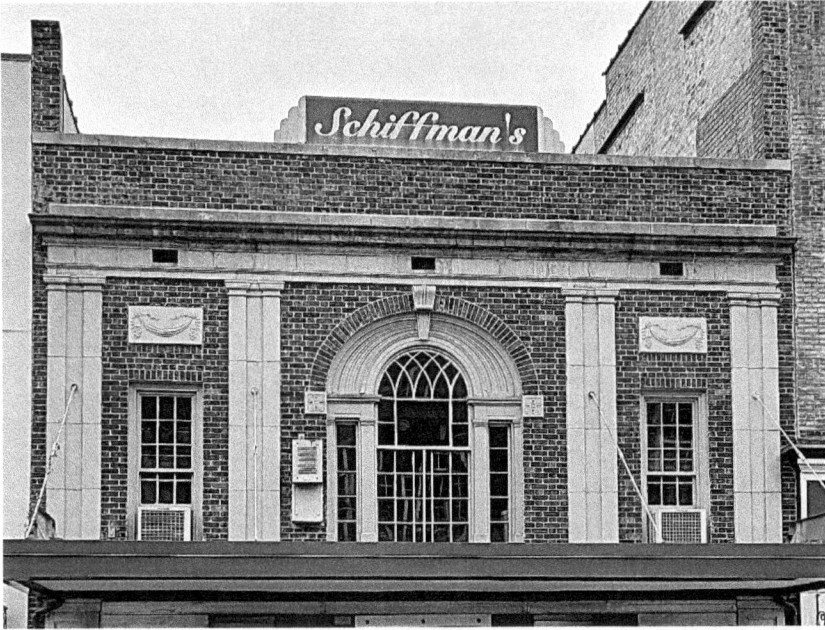

Schiffman's downtown and Friendly Center stores. *Author photos*

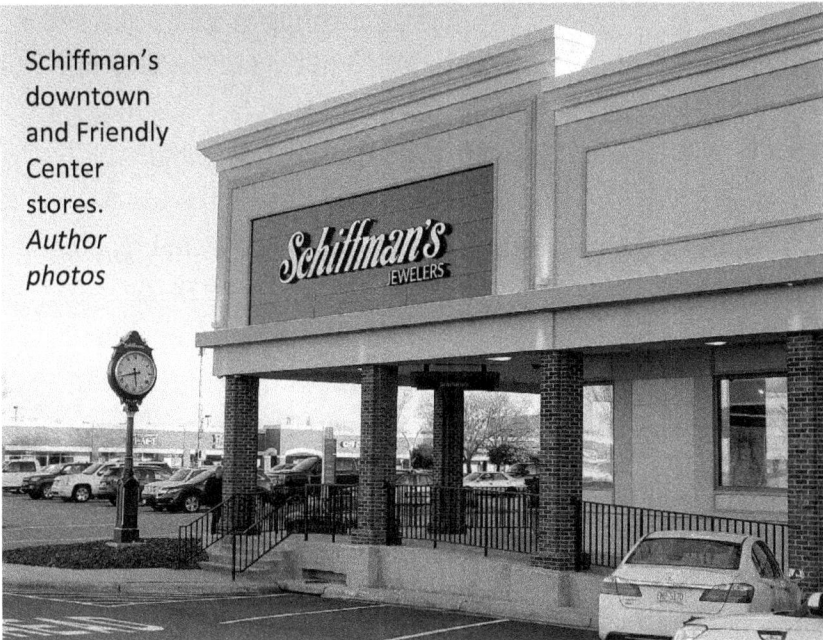

Retail

Schiffman's Jewelers, which had opened downtown in 1893, added a 4,000-square-foot store at Friendly Center.

1972

Billy Cunningham led the Carolina Cougars to the ABA Finals in 1972.

Basketball

The Carolina Cougars came into their own, vaulting to the top of the Eastern Division standings in their first season under Larry Brown, finishing at 57-27.

Billy Cunningham led the team, averaging 24.1 points and 12 rebounds a game, with Mack Calvin scoring at a 17.5 clip and Joe Caldwell averaging 16.7. In fact, six Cougars all averaged in double figures for the top offensive team in the league in 1972-73.

Brown was named ABA Coach of the Year, and Cunningham was chosen as the league MVP. The team's attendance was up, too, as a record 340,000 fans passed through the turnstiles. On December 30, a crowd of 14,126 turned out for a 104-91 victory over the Kentucky Colonels in Greensboro.

In the playoffs, the Cougars kept rolling at first, defeating the New York Nets 4 games to 1 before meeting Kentucky for the championship. The team took a 3-games-to-2 lead and needed just one more win for the title, but the Colonels turned the tables by winning the last two to claim the championship.

Cinema

Quaker Village Theatres gave Greensboro its second twin cinema when it opened at Dolly Madison Road and West Friendly Avenue just before Christmas. *The Valachi Papers* with Charles Bronson and *1776* with Ken Howard were the opening attractions.

The theater operated until 2003.

Music

The King held court at the Greensboro Coliseum. It was Elvis Presley's first of five appearances at the venue over the next five years, with the last coming April 21, 1977, just four months before his death.

1973

Aviation

Six people died when a twin-engine Cessna crashed in a wooded field just after takeoff at Greensboro-High Point-Salem Regional Airport.

The weather was good, and skies were clear. The pilot radioed the control tower just after takeoff, but that was the last that was heard of him. The plane crashed just two minutes later and exploded, causing a small fire that was quickly extinguished.

Basketball

The Carolina Cougars fielded another strong offensive team, ranking second in the ABA, but they failed to match the success of their previous season, slipping to 47-37 and third place in the Eastern Division.

Billy Cunningham again led the team in scoring at 20.5 a game, and in hauled down a team-best 10.3 rebounds for good measure, as seven Cougars averaged in double figures scoring. But Cunningham appeared in just 32 games thanks to a kidney problem that required surgery in December. When the Cougars hit the playoffs, they were no match for the Kentucky Colonels, who swept them in four games in the first round.

That series marked the end of the team's run in North Carolina, as the Cougars were sold and moved to St. Louis in the offseason. The team, renamed the Spirits of St. Louis, played its last two seasons in Missouri and failed to post a winning record either year.

Community

The Greensboro Zoo opened at Country Park. It would expand two years later to include bear, bobcat, and puma exhibits.

Music

Elton John played the Greensboro Coliseum on September 21 in support of his album *Goodbye Yellow Brick Road*. A ticket in the orchestra section could be had for $5.

John took the stage just a day after singer-songwriter Jim Croce died in a plane crash. As a tribute, John walked down a runway to a piano illuminated by a spotlight and played his hit song "Daniel."

The song, about a friend who's been lost, begins with the line "Daniel is traveling tonight on a plane..."

The vacant Kroger superstore in 2022. *Author photo*

Retail

Kroger opened its first Greensboro "superstore" at 3950 West Market Street. A second would follow a year later in the new Palmer Plaza Shopping Center at 3109 Yanceyville Street. ...

Carolina Curlz started out as the Flower Pot, a drive-up florist. *Author photo*

The Flower Pot, the city's first drive-in florist, opened on Holden Road. Built by Grier Hunt, it was shaped like, well, a flower pot. In spite of this, however, it has spent most of its history as a hair salon. Adam Farmer started cutting hair there when he took over in 1980.

As of 2022 it was called Classic Curlz.

1974

Basketball

The Atlantic Coast Conference men's basketball tournament featured the first- and fourth-ranked teams in the nation.

North Carolina State and Maryland both played up to their billing in the championship game, as the Greensboro Coliseum hosted one of the most memorable games in NCAA history. No. 4 Maryland made 61 percent of its shots — and still wound up on the losing end of a 103-100 score against the top-ranked Wolfpack.

The Terrapins made 12 of their first 14 shots as they raced out to a 25-12 lead. But N.C. State closed the gap to 55-50 at halftime, then went on a 16-6 run to open the second half. The Wolfpack, who shot 55 percent on the game themselves, couldn't close things out, though.

Maryland actually had a chance to win on the final possession twice, but the Terps couldn't get a good look at the basket at the end of regulation and turned the ball over trailing 101-100 while trying to set up the final shot in overtime.

Phil Spence's bucket, which put the Wolfpack ahead, and two free throws by Monte Towe sealed the victory.

Tom Burleson, the Wolfpack's 7-foot-2 center, led the way

with 38 points and 13 rebounds, while ACC Player of the Year David Thompson added 29 points in the victory. ...

The Greensboro Coliseum hadn't seen the last of college basketball in 1974, because it went on to host its only NCAA men's basketball Final Four — a tournament that was even more memorable because North Carolina State won it all.

The Wolfpack earned a trip to the finals in their first game at Greensboro by defeating UCLA 80-77 in the semifinals before 15,500 fans.

It wasn't easy, though.

The game took two overtimes, and the Wolfpack — who had lost by 18 points to the Bruins earlier in the season — had to climb back from an 11-point deficit midway through the second half to force overtime.

UCLA led 74-67 in the second overtime before N.C. State star David Thompson powered a comeback, scoring a bucket with just under 3 minutes left that cut UCLA's lead to four points. Then, with less than a minute on the clock, he hit the go-ahead basket and added a pair of free throws to ice the game. Thompson finished with 28 points and 10 rebounds as N.C. State won for the 29th time in 30 games.

It marked the first time in eight years (and just the second time in 11) that the Bruins weren't crowned champions.

"I have known the streak wouldn't go on forever," UCLA coach John Wooden said. "We're just glad it went on as long as it did."

But the Wolfpack weren't done.
They went on to defeat third-ranked Marquette 76-64 in the championship game, as Thompson scored 21 points in a game that was never really close after halftime. The Wolfpack built a 39-30 lead at intermission and stretched that to 54-33 less

than six minutes into the second half.

Thompson, who led all scorers in the tournament with 97 points, was named Most Outstanding Player.

Retail

A discount supermarket called Food Town opened at the Golden Gate Center, in a former Kroger location. Its slogan was a six-letter string of initials, LFPINC, which stood for "Lowest Food Prices in North Carolina."

The concept proved successful enough to expand to six locations in Greensboro by the end of the decade. Two of them in were former Kmart Foods stores, a failed concept that the discount chain abandoned in 1975.

In 1982, the chain got a new name, still recognizable today: Food Lion.

1975

Retail

Four Seasons Mall, the city's first indoor mall, opened off High Point Road. A total of 95 stores were spread out over two levels and 900,000 square feet.

The mall's location at the new Interstate 40 and U.S. 29 (High Point Road, known as Gate City Boulevard since 2013) made it an ideal focal point for customers. J.C. Penney had opened as the first anchor in October of 1974, followed by Belk in February 1975, with Greensboro-based Meyer's as the third main store.

Other stores served as secondary anchors: Frankenberger's, McCrory's, Miller & Rhoads, and Thalhimers, along with a Winn-Dixie supermarket and Eckerd Drugs.

Shoppers leave the Four Seasons Mall in 2022. *Author photo*

1976

Community

The Edward R. Zane Planetarium opened at the science center, named for the civic leader who also served as mayor of Hamilton Lakes before it was annexed by Greensboro. He also mediated discussions between students and local business leaders during the Woolworth and Kress lunch counter sit-in protests.

The planetarium, with a capacity of 87 people, reopened in 2013 as the OmniSphere, a fully domed globe venue at 4301 Lawndale Drive.

The Greensboro Science Center. *Author photo*

Music

Country music star Emmylou Harris returned to Greensboro for a concert in April at the Piedmont Sports Arena.

Harris was a Birmingham native, but she'd received a scholarship to the School of Music, Theatre, and Dance at the University of North Carolina at Greensboro. While there, she had appeared in *The Tempest* by William Shakespeare and a children's production of *The Dancing Donkey*.

She also formed a folk duo with UNC-Chapel Hill graduate Mike Williams called The Emerald City, performing songs by the Everly Brothers, Bob Dylan, and others at local clubs and other venues as far up the coast as Washington, D.C.

Although she ultimately chose music over drama and left college for New York City, her connection to Greensboro remained — and was reaffirmed when she returned for her birthday April 2.

The Chamber of Commerce proclaimed it Emmylou Harris Day and threw her a "welcome back party" attended by college friends and former professors.

Emmylou Harris, right, visits the University of North Carolina at Greensboro in 1976.

Over her career, Harris would record some 30 albums, releasing her first in 1969. Her major label debut, *Pieces of the Sky*, came just a year before her return to Greensboro, with her single "If I Could Only Win Your Love" reaching No. 4 on the country chart.

Her follow-up album, *Elite Hotel*, would reach No. 1, and so would her album *Trio* with Linda Ronstadt and Dolly Parton. She had a pair of No. 1 singles the year she returned to Greensboro — "Together Again" and "Sweet Dreams" — then hit the top of the charts three more times after that.

Retail

A year after its first indoor mall opened, Greensboro welcomed a second: the two-story Carolina Circle at Highway 29 North and Cone Boulevard.

Belk, one of three main anchors, was the first to open in February at the 750,000-square-foot center. Montgomery Ward and Ivey's (later Dillard's) were the other two big department stores.

Another big attraction was a skating rink, which opened in June, but the grand opening wasn't until August 4. That's when 22 stores opened, with 50 more due to follow in the ensuing months.

Mayor Ray Brantley touted the skating rink as a way to appeal to kids, similar to the play areas at McDonald's: "The housewife spends most of the disposable income in the family. And who controls the housewife? The kids. It's true. We want this to be a pleasant place for kids to be."

Other tenants at Carolina Circle over the years would include Piccadilly Cafeteria, Camelot Records, Waldenbooks, Texas Jeans, and Radio Shack — one of the original tenants. It stayed at the mall until it closed in 1996, to be replaced by Shalimar Photography.

The mall was also the site of Greensboro's first multiplex cinema, which had six screens from which to choose. The Carolina Circle Mall 6 was also the first AMC theater in North Carolina. Located on the mall's lower level next to a Hallmark shop and across from the Piccadilly Cafeteria, it opened on November 12 showing *Alex and the Gypsy*; *The Next Man*; *Not Now, Darling*; *Scorchy*; *Superbug: Super Agent*, and *Two Minute Warning*.

The entire mall was torn down in 2002. The site now is home to a Super Walmart.

1977

Retail

Three deer took fright at the sound of cleaning equipment in the parking lot at Carolina Circle Mall and made a run for it — directly through two plate-glass windows. The unfortunate animals then fell 18 feet to the floor of the mall beside the ice rink.

Amazingly, two of them survived and were captured, then released. The third, sadly, died of a broken neck.

1979

Baseball

Greensboro had a new baseball team, the Hornets, playing in the Class A Western Carolinas League. The team placed fourth, but attendance was encouraging, as the Cincinnati Reds affiliate drew an average of 2,435 fans a game.

Cinema

A four-screen multiplex called General Cinemas opened at Four Seasons Mall with a total of 1,100 seats. It remained open until 2001, when it was closed to make way for a mall expansion project.

Violence

Liberal activists from Durham, many of them formerly part of the anti-war and civil rights movements, created a Workers Viewpoint Organization (WVO) to advocate for labor.

They believed so strongly in their cause that some gave up jobs as professors and doctors so they could move to Greensboro.

Why?

They thought they could best advocate for workers' rights by taking jobs at the Cone Mills textile factories and galvanizing union support there. But their activities weren't limited to union organizing. They also spoke out for racial equality and against police brutality, among other things.

Racial divisions, they believed, pitted Black and white workers against each other, hindering them from pursuing their common interests of better wages and working conditions. This made the Ku Klux Klan a natural target for protests the WVO organized in response to KKK violence in Decatur, Illinois, and elsewhere.

On July 8, the Klan announced plans to show a white supremacist movie in China Grove (about an hour southwest of Greensboro), the WVO organized a protest march that ended in a standoff: Armed Klansmen stood on the front porch of the town hall, while WVO members chanted, waved bats, and burned a Confederate flag.

Police arrived and forced the Klan members back inside, but it wasn't the end of the tensions.

The WVO changed its name to the more combative Communist Workers Party (CWP), and decided to march through the low-income Morningside Homes neighborhood of Greensboro. The march, provocatively dubbed "Death to the Klan" was promoted by fliers, one of which called for Klan members to by beaten and driven out of town.

Nelson Johnson, who'd been involved in the Dudley High protests a decade earlier, applied for the parade permit.

The CWP then taunted the KKK with "an open letter" to the group and its sympathizers, declaring the rally's intention to "organize and to physically smash the racist KKK wherever it rears its ugly head," adding that "we challenge you to attend our November 3rd rally in Greensboro."

The KKK — now joined by members of the American Nazi Party — responded with its own threat to "traitors" that "even now the cross-hairs are on the back of YOUR necks."

Johnson's involvement may have complicated things. Police didn't care for him, and the feeling was mutual (he said he expected them to keep up their "slimy tactics" ahead of the march). The police department, perhaps unsurprisingly, didn't say anything to the CWP about the Klan's threats.

On the morning of November 3, the Klansmen and Nazis assembled in a caravan and headed out to Morningside Homes, where the CWP marchers had gathered. The marchers started beating on the KKK cars with their pickets, and the Klansmen responded by pulling guns out of the trunk of one of their cars.

Then the shooting started.

By the time it was over, four CWP protesters were dead and a fifth was fatally wounded. Among them was a woman named Sandi Smith who'd taken children to hide behind the porch at the community center. When she stepped out to look for other children, she was shot above the eye and died immediately.

A funeral march a week later drew 500 participants despite the rainy weather. Their numbers were matched by those of National Guard members checking weapons and looking for signs of more violence. Between 2,000 and 5,000 others lined the parade route.

Several people were caught on tape shooting at protesters, and five of them were charged with murder. But a total of 78 potential jurors were dismissed, mostly for admitting they wouldn't have been able to judge a KKK member objectively. When the dust cleared on the selection process, an all-white jury was empaneled, including an anti-communist Cuban exile.

The jury took a week to deliver not-guilty verdicts in all five cases.

A federal trial before another all-white jury produced the same result, although the survivors were awarded damages in civil cases involving three of the victims. They'd asked for $48 million, but the largest award, for the wrongful death of Marty Nathan, was $351,500.

It wasn't until more than 40 years later that the Greensboro City Council, in a 7-2 vote, passed a resolution acknowledging that the police hadn't sought to stop or detain Klansmen and Nazis, even though they knew they were armed. They also, the resolution said, "failed to warn the marchers of their extensive foreknowledge of the racist, violent attack planned against the marchers by members of the Ku Klux Klan and the American Nazi Party with the assistance of a paid GPD informant."

Nelson Johnson welcomed the decision in an interview with CNN.

"My children have had to grow up on the cultural view in this city that I was an evil person, that I set this up, that I knew it was going to happen and that I wanted a fight with the Klan and so forth," he said. "Just a lot of nonsense but I think that has cleared up a little bit now and we're given a little more credit for trying to do the right thing."

Council member Michelle Kennedy called the apology "41 years too late."

The incident is still known today as the Greensboro Massacre.

The Skyline Rises

1980-1989

Renaissance Plaza, built in 1989, became one of the city's tallest buildings upon completion. *Author photo*

1980

Baseball

After one season in the Western Carolinas League, Greensboro made its debut in the South Atlantic League and took it by storm. The Hornets — now a New York Yankees affiliate — won the North Division with an 82-67 record, then beat the Gastonia Cardinals 2 games to 1 and swept the Charleston Royals in three games to claim the title.

Future Yankees star Don Mattingly hit .358 to claim the batting championship by a wide margin over teammate Matt Winters (.320) and drove in 105 runs. The Hornets averaged 3,671 fans per game, the best for any Greensboro team in history — although they would top that figure next year.

Milestones

Greensboro's growth moderated to just 8 percent during the 1970s, reaching 155,642 by the end of that decade.

1981

Baseball

Even without Don Mattingly, the Greensboro Hornets were a force to be reckoned with, posting a league-best 98-43 record and winning the championship series 3 games to 2 over the Greenville Pirates.

Fire

A fire caused significant damage to the Carolina Theatre, but the building was saved.

Suspicion fell on a 47-year-old woman named Melvaleene Reva Ferguson, whose body was found after being burned at temperatures of more than 2,000 degrees.

Ferguson, who had a long history of emotional distress, had been seen near the theater stairwell around 10 a.m. working with cloth materials. She was believed to have set it on fire with a match, and the flames spread upward toward the third-floor balcony before it could be contained.

Ferguson's ghost is believed by some to haunt the building.

Aggie Stadium, now Truist Stadium, opened in 1981.
Author photo

Football

Aggie Stadium (since renamed Truist Stadium), a 17,500-seat outdoor facility opened at North Carolina A&T. The stadium was designed by architect W. Edward Jenkins, a university alumnus. Until this time, A&T had played at World War Memorial Stadium.

Government

John W. Forbis began a six-year (three-term) run as mayor.

1982

Aviation

A new terminal complex was finished at Greensboro–High Point–Winston-Salem Regional Airport.

Baseball

The Greensboro Hornets were champions for the third straight season following a 3-2 series victory over the Florence Blue Jays. They again had the league's best regular-season record too, finishing at 96-45.

The Hornets would advance to the finals a few more times but would never again claim the league title.

1983

Basketball

Greensboro's Page High School capped an unbeaten season by defeating Goldsboro for the state championship 73-59 at the Coliseum. Tournament MVP Haywood Jeffires scored 21 points, and Danny Manning added 19 for the Pirates.

Manning averaged 18.8 points a game on the season as the Pirates compiled a perfect 26-0 record.

He would go on to star at the University of Kansas and become the first overall pick in the 1988 NBA draft, playing in the NBA from 1988 to 2003 and later embarking on a coaching career. Jeffires, however, took a different path: He focused on football at North Carolina State and was a first-round draft pick in 1987.

He played 10 seasons in the NFL, with his best year coming in 1991: He led the league in receptions with 100 catches for 1,181 yards and seven touchdowns. ...

Playing at the Greensboro Coliseum, Michael Jordan had his highest-scoring college game. His 39 points led North Carolina to a 72-65 win over Georgia Tech.

1984

Journalism

Greensboro's two daily newspapers formally merged into a single morning publication called the *Greensboro News & Record*.

1985

Music

Bruce Springsteen drew more than 30,000 fans to a two-night engagement January 18 and 19 at the Greensboro Coliseum.

Weather

The temperature fell to 8 below zero on January 21, the coldest reading ever in Greensboro.

1987

Aviation

Greensboro–High Point–Winston-Salem Regional Airport was renamed Piedmont Triad International Airport.

Government

Vic Nusbaum Jr. was elected to the first of three consecutive mayoral terms.

Retail

Four Seasons Mall expanded, opening a third floor of shops to bring its selection to 200 stores. Now with more than

1 million square feet of space, the mall also changed its name to Four Seasons Town Centre. ...

The last Greensboro A&P closed, ending a 78-year run in the city. During that time, the company operated 42 locations at one time or another.

1988

Cinema

The Greensboro Beef Burger made an appearance in the movie *Bull Durham*, when the Durham Bulls went to play in Greensboro.

Music

The Blind Tiger opened at its original location, a former A&P store on Walker Avenue at Elam in Lindley Park. The corner had long been a mini-hub of activity.

The A&P had been there as far back as 1930. There was a Suds and Duds coin-op laundry, a barbershop, and Elam Pharmacy, which had a soda fountain.

But the character of the neighborhood had changed in the late 1940s when the city closed Walker Avenue through the Woman's College of the University of North Carolina, which wanted to build a library. The barbershop stayed open, but many of the other businesses closed up or moved on.

Sno-White Cleaners around the corner on Elam has been open for more than six decades. But the Blind Tiger and the other bars and nightclubs in the area, such as Wahoo's, have defined the area in more recent years. Neil Reitzel and Scott Toben opened the bar in 1988 in the former A&P, although it has since moved down the road to 1819 Spring Garden in 2011.

The Blind Tiger's original location at Elam and Walker, top, and its current building. *Author photos*

Over the years, it has hosted the likes of Hootie and the Blowfish; Edwin McCain; Little Feat; and Ben Folds Five, from nearby Winston-Salem — in their first show. (They would soon have a hit with "Brick.")

Sno-White Cleaners on Elam has been in business for more than six decades. *Author photo*

Retail

In an effort to keep up with Four Seasons, Carolina Circle Mall undertook a $6 million renovation that included better lighting and a $250,000 carousel built especially for the venue.

Another update was less popular: The mall closed the skating rink (the only one in Greensboro) and replaced it with a food court.

1989

Business

The Jefferson Standard Building had been the tallest in Greensboro for 66 years, but within two years' time, four buildings would surpass it.

Two would be built in 1989: the 19-story Renaissance Plaza (256 feet tall) at 230 North Elm Street and the 21-story Wells Fargo Tower at 300 North Green Street, which took the mantle as the city's tallest building at just over 328 feet.

It would retain that distinction for just a single year, until the Lincoln Financial Building surpassed it.

The Wells Fargo Tower became the city's tallest building in 1989, eclipsing the Jefferson Standard Building, which had held the honor for 66 years, but that title lasted for only about a year. *Author photo*

Brassfield Cinema, a 10-screen multiplex, began more than three decades in business at the Brassfield Shopping Center in 1989. *Author photo*

Cinema

The 10-screen Brassfield Cinema opened on October 6 in the Brassfield Shopping Center with total seating of 1,700. It remained open until closing in March of 2020 amid the COVID pandemic. The closure would become permanent the following spring.

Ice Hockey

A new team called the Greensboro Monarchs made a splash as hockey returned to a town that had been without a team since the Generals folded 12 years earlier.

The Monarchs won the East Coast Hockey League title in their first season, finishing fourth in the regular season with a 29-27 record before catching fire during the playoffs. They upset the third-place Virginia Lancers in the first round, 3 games to 1, then shocked the Erie Panthers, who had finished the season tied for first place, 2 games to 0 in the semifinals.

The best-of-seven championship series pitted them

against Winston-Salem, which had tied Erie atop the standings. The series was tied at one game apiece before the Monarchs reeled off three straight wins to claim the championship.

They made the finals twice more in their six-year history, but they never won another title. Despite their best average attendance and a third appearance in the championship series, 1994-95 turned out to be their last year in the ECHL.

Control tower at Piedmont Triad International Airport. *Author photo*

Athletes and Attractions

1990–1999

The Lincoln Financial Building became the tallest building in Greensboro upon its completion in 1990. *Author photo*

1990

Business

The 20-story Lincoln Financial Building was competed. At 374 feet, it became the tallest building in Greensboro.

Cinema

Litchfield Cinemas 7 opened at High Point and Groomtown roads September 28. It became a Regal cinema four years later and, in 2002, was renamed Sedgefield Crossing $2 Cinemas, showing second-run films.

The Bellemeade Street Deck parking structure rose on the site of the original O. Henry Hotel. *Author photo*

Community

The Bellemeade Street Deck parking structure opened with 500 parking spaces on four floors at Greene and Bellemeade — site of the original O. Henry Hotel.

When completed, it would be eight stories tall with room for 1,276 cars. ...

The Greensboro Cultural Center and Festival Park, together a $8.5 million project, opened downtown.

The center began in 1980 as the Visual Arts Center, housed in a 1924 building at Friendly Avenue and Davie Street.

The city purchased it or $238,000 and used a federal grant of more than half a million dollars to transform the space. It was expanded to become the Cultural Arts Center using a $6 million bond and a $1 million donation from the United Arts Council.

The resulting center was spread over several buildings: the

Entrance to the Greensboro Cultural Center. *Author photo*

former Greensboro Daily News building, a timber mill, the old WFMY-Channel 2 building, and the former Greensboro Spring Air Mattress Company building.

In 2000, one estimate put the number of visitors at 100,000 a month.

Milestones

Greensboro's population surged by 18.2 percent to 183,894. It would be well past 200,000 — and still climbing — by the end of the decade.

1991

Crime

Robbers at Carolina Circle shot and wounded a 54-year-old man as he left Montgomery Ward with his two daughters.

The Sheraton Greensboro Hotel is across from the Four Seasons mall. *Author photo*

Lodging

The Sheraton Greensboro Hotel at Four Seasons opened as the tallest hotel in the city and third-tallest building overall, behind the Lincoln Financial Building and Wells Fargo Tower. It had more stories than either at 28 and rose 270 feet tall.

Music

The Grateful Dead played two shows at the Greensboro Coliseum, with more than 29,000 fans in attendance.

1992

Golf

Davis Love III won the Greater Greensboro Open by six strokes, the first of three widely spaced wins (1992, 2006, and 2015), putting him second all-time behind Sam Snead.

1993

Baseball

Future Hall of Famer Derek Jeter played for the Greensboro Hornets, helping them to a first-place finish in the North Division and a spot in the finals, where they fell to the Savannah Cardinals 3 games to 2.

Jeter hit .395 on the season and made the All-Star team at shortstop.

Community

Renovations increased the Greensboro Coliseum arena's seating capacity to 23,500.

Government

Carolyn S. Allen began a three-term tenure as mayor, serving through 1999.

She was the first woman to lead the city.

1994

Baseball

Greensboro's New York Yankees affiliate in the South Atlantic League got a new name, the Bats, but the team never managed to win a championship before changing its name again (to the Grasshoppers) in 2005.

1995

Football

Aggie Stadium at North Carolina A&T was expanded, with 5,000 seats being added to the south end zone.

Ice Hockey

Greensboro had a team called the Carolina Monarchs in the American Hockey League starting in 1995; it lasted two years amid declining attendance and never made the playoffs.

The Monarchs made history, however, on January 18, 1997, when they set an AHL attendance record in a 5-4 win over the Kentucky Thoroughblades at the Greensboro Coliseum. A crowd of 20,672 showed up for the contest.

1996

Gymnastics

The U.S. women's gymnastics team held training sessions at the Greensboro Coliseum in preparation for the Summer Olympics in Atlanta.

1997

Ice Hockey

Greensboro had a National Hockey League team to call its own, even if the situation was only temporary.

The Hartford Whalers moved to town as the Carolina Hurricanes, playing at the Greensboro Coliseum for two seasons until their permanent home in Raleigh could be finished.

The Hurricanes dropped a 4-3 decision to the Pittsburgh Penguins before 18,661 fans in their first game at the Coliseum.

1998

Retail

Belk and Dillard's closed up shop at Carolina Circle, leaving Montgomery Ward as the mall's only anchor. The mall would be demolished six years later.

1999

Baseball

Scott Seabol set league records with a 35-game hitting streak and 55 doubles in his third season with Greensboro, but the Bats could do no better than second in the Sally League Central Division and were eliminated by the Capital City Bombers 2 games to 1 in the playoffs.

Golf

Jesper Parnevik finished 23 under par to set a tournament

record at the Greater Greensboro Chrysler Classic. The event was held at Forest Oaks, its home from 1977 to 2007.

Government

Keith Holliday was elected to the first of four terms as mayor.

Ice Hockey

A new version of the Greensboro Generals began play in the East Coast Hockey League. The team would last five seasons, making the playoffs just once, in 2002-03, when they posted a record of 42-21 and lost in the second round.

Music

In just 78 minutes, all 22,450 tickets to see the Backstreet Boys at the Coliseum were gone. The event set an attendance record for the venue at the time and grossed more than $1 million in ticket sales.

Retail

Kroger, a mainstay in Greensboro since 1952, exited the city in a swap with Harris Teeter — which gave up several stores in Virginia and took over the former Kroger properties in Greensboro. Kroger would eventually purchase the entire Harris Teeter chain, but the stores in Greensboro continued to operate under that name.

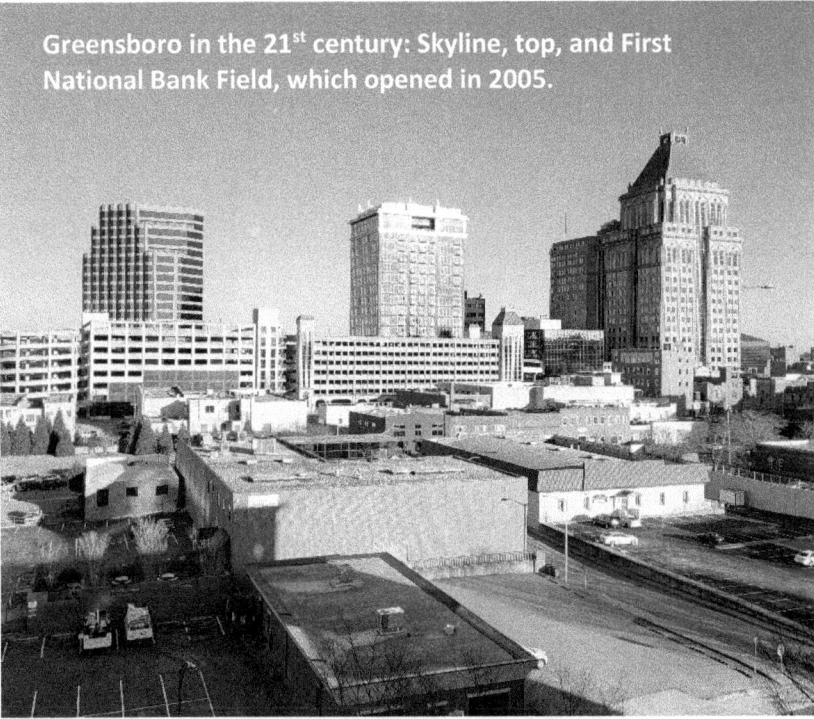

Greensboro in the 21st century: Skyline, top, and First National Bank Field, which opened in 2005.

Downtown views, with Center City Park above. *Author photo*

Greensboro water tower off Interstate 73, part of the
Greensboro Urban Loop. *Author photo*

References

"4 slain at anti-Klan rally buried after march," Fort Worth Star-Telegram, p. 4, Nov. 12, 1979.

"6 Greensboro Policemen Shot In Street Ambush," Durham Sun, p. 1, May 23, 1969.

"35 Things You Probably Didn't Know About Greensboro, NC," movoto.com.

"60 Years of Science," greensborosciencecenter.wordpress.com, Sept. 29, 2017.

"70 Things You Might Not Know About WFMY News 2 As We Celebrate 70 Years,"
        wfmynews2.com, May 6, 2019.

"301 S. Elm Street Guilford Building," library.greensboro-nc.gov.

"1969 Greensboro uprising explained," everything.explained.today.

"2017 Watch List Represents Diverse Issues and Concerns," preservationgreensboro.org.

"A&T Student Killed; Curfew Declared," High Point Enterprise, p. 1, May 22, 1969.

"ABA Franchise Will Be Carolina Cougars," Burlington Daily Times-News, p. 11, April 1, 1969.

"About Cone Mill Villages," triadhistory.org.

"About Us," greensborocc.org.

Alicoate, Jack (editor). "The 1939 Radio Annual," The Radio Daily, 1939.

Alyta, Ken. "Title Dream Comes True For Wolfpack," Lumberton Robesonian, p. 7,
        March 26, 1974.

"American Top 40 Radio Station Surveys New Hampshire Thru North Dakota,"
        kimsloans.wordpress.com.

"The A&P Comes to Greensboro," groceteria.com, May 27, 2018.

"The Answer is Three Miles," Greensboro Telegram, p. 2, March 31, 1911.

"An Appreciation of an Honored Citizen," Greensboro Patriot, p. 2, April 13, 1914.

"Around The City," Raleigh News and Observer, p. 14, July 30, 1929.

"Bank Receives in its New Skyscraper," Raleigh News and Observer, p. 11, Oct. 2, 1927.

Barkley, Meredith. "Odd Architecture," greensboro.com, March 9, 1996.

Barron, Richard. "100-year-old Greensboro factory's new look holds on to the past,"
        greensboro.com, April 12, 2018.

"Baseball in Greensboro Through the Years," greensboro.com, Jan. 23, 2015.

Baseballreference.com.

Basketball-reference.com.

'Beef Burger," biff-burger.com.

"Benjamin Cone," findagrave.com.

"Betty Jameson Fires Final Round 70 To Win Open," Durham Morning Herald, p. 6,
        June 30, 1947.

Biondi, Martha. "The Black Revolution on Campus," University of California Press, 2012.

Bledsoe, Jerry. "The Story of Hardee's," ourstate.com, May 27, 2021.

theblindtiger.com

"Bowling Alley Burns," Durham Morning Herald, p. 2, Feb. 17, 1961.

"A brief history of Lexington-style barbecue," barbecuebros.co.

Brasier, John. "Cafeteria leftovers slow construction of downtown hotel," Triad Business Journal,
        bizjournals.com, Jan. 7, 2020.

Briggs, Benjamin. "An Old Place, A New Look," preservationgreensboro.org, May 29, 2009.

Briggs, Benjamin. "Is This Landmark Irving Park's Oldest House?" preservationgreensboro.org,
        Oct. 30, 2015.

Brooks, Bob. "Seven Schools Form Atlantic Coast Conference," Raleigh News and Observer,
        p. 13,
        June 15, 1953.

"Brutalism," designingbuildings.co.uk, Jan. 7, 2022

"Cadets, Irish Protect Win Streaks in Upset Week," Salinas Californian, p.13, Oct. 2, 1950.

Calhoon, Robert M. "Immanuel College," ncpedia.org, 2006.

"Cancelled – Walking Tour of Grimsley High School Campus," preservationgreensboro.org,
        June 24, 2020.

"Carolina Cadillac Company Building, 304 East Market Street," pocketsights.com.

"Carolina Cougars," remembertheaba.com.

Catallo, Cara. "The Heart of the Arts/Greensboro Cultural Center's 10th Anniversary," greensboro.com, Sept. 9, 2000.

"Center Thatre, Greensboro, N.C., 1949," Going to the Show, gtts.oasis.unc.edu.

"Charles W. Irvin Sr.," Durham Morning Herald, p. 2, Jan. 26, 1960.

Choate, Paul. "Ralph Havis, owner of Beef Burger in Greensboro, dies at 78," myfox8.com, July 15, 2021.

Cinematreasures.org.

"A City of Change," greensboro.com, Sept, 13, 2013.

"City of Greensboro and the Gillespie Park Golf Club, Incorporated, Appellants, v. George Simkins, Jr., Phillip W. Cook, Leonidas Wolf, Samuel Murray, Arthur Lee, Jr., Lonnie Reynolds, William Holmes, Elijah Herring, Joseph Studivent and James G. Hagins, Appellees, 246 F.2d 425 (4th Cir. 1957)," law.justia.com.

"Civic leader Edward Zane dies at 91," greensboro.com, June 24, 1991.

"Club History," starmountforest.com.

"Cone Mills Corporation Records, 1858-1997," finding-aids.lib.unc.edu.

"Congratulations," Greensboro Daily News, p. 4, April 29, 1921.

Corbett, Warren. "Tom Alston," sabr.org.

Davis, Chanel. "Mike Clark and The Mill get ready to give Greensboro another facelift," yesweekly.com, Nov. 8, 2017.

"Dinkler Hotels," southernedition.com.

"Doors of the O. Henry Will be Opened to Public Today," Greensboro Daily News, p. 1, July 2, 1919.

Ebrahimji, Alisha. "Decades after Klansmen killed 5 during protest, a North Carolina city's apology comes too late for some," cnn.com, Oct. 14, 2020.

"Edwin A. Morris," historync.org.

Ellis, Cady. "Overseas Replacement Depot," ncpedia.org, 2006.

"Emmylou Harris: From UNCG to the Grand Ole Opry," Spartan Stories, uncghistory.blogspot.com, Dec. 14, 2015.

"The Ellis-Stone Department Store, 207 South Elm Street," pocketsights.com.

"Encyclopedia of Southern Jewish Communities - Greensboro, North Carolina," isjl.org.

"Explosion at oil refinery in N.C. kills one person," Greenwood (S.C.) Index-Journal, gendisasters.com, Aug. 23, 1955.

Evans, Linda. "Passport to History," Greensboro History Museum Journal, May/June 2007.

Eye, Billy. "Tippling and Tenpin," ohenrymag.com, August 2021.

Eye, Billy. "You Auto Be in Pictures," ohenrymag.com, September 2020.

"Former MLK Jr. home offers tours, shoebox lunches," Statesville Record and Landmark, p. A4, Jan. 28, 2021.

Friedlander, Brett. "Wolfpack Flashback: State Beats Maryland in ACC's Greatest Game," si.com, March 14, 2020.

Garrity, John. "He's Manning For The Future," Sports Illustrated, Oct. 17, 1983.

"Gardner's Wins Duckpin Title," Charlotte Observer, p. 6-B, April 23, 1957.

"Gary Sharp Top Scorer For Generals," Burlington Daily Times-News, p. 4B, March 5, 1963.

"Gens Could Break Open EHL Battle," High Point Enterprise, p. 10, Jan. 8, 1963.

Gilmer Bros. ad, Greensboro Daily News, p. 10, Sept. 10, 1915.

Gleiter, Sue. "Throwback Thursday: Remember Uncle John's Pancake House and its lengthy pancake menu?" pennlive.com, May 29, 2014.

"The Ghost Mall," otherstream.com, Nov. 18, 1999.

"Greensboro and the Concrete Jungle," preservationgreensboro.org.

"Greensboro's Beef Burger restaurant permanently closes," wxii12.com, May 21, 2021.

"Greensboro Building Shows Good Advance," Raleigh News and Observer, p. 12, Jan. 4, 1927.

"Greensboro City Directory, 1913-14," archive.org.

"Greensboro (Guilford County, N.C.) city directory, 1930," archive.org.

"Greensboro, N.C. Directory 1915-16 including Proximity, Revolution Mills and White Oak Mills," libcdm1.uncg.edu.

"Greensboro Country Club," Twin City Daily Sentinel (Winston-Salem), p. 10, Sept. 23, 1911.

"Greensboro Crash Kills Six," Burlington Daily Times News, gendisasters.com, April 4, 1973.

"Greensboro Generals (1959-1977)," funwhileitlasted.net.

"Greensboro's Greatest Fire," Greensboro Patriot, p. 3, Jan. 27, 1904.

"Greensboro Masonic Temple," greensboromasonicmuseum.org.

"Greensboro's Race to the Sky," preservationgreensboro.org.

"Greensboro Science Center Omnisphere," aplf-planetariums.org.

"Greensboro Weather Records," extremeweatherwatch.com.

Griffis, Matthew. "Carnegie Negro Library, Greensboro, North Carolina (1924-1963)," blackpast.org, Nov. 17, 2019.

Groceteria.com.

"Hamilton Lakes and Parks," hamiltonstarmount.org.

"Handsome Building," Greensboro Telegram, p. 4, July 25, 1901.

Hicks, Gayle. "A Brief History of Greensboro," greensboro-nc.gov, 1997.

"High Court Gets Greensboro Golf Segregation Case," Durham Morning Herald, p. 11, April 9, 1957.

Highwayhost.org.

"Hill's Greensboro City Directory, 1934," libcdm1.uncg.edu.

"Hill's Greensboro City Directory, 1942," ancestraltrackers.net.

"Hill's Greensboro City Directory, 1962," libcdm1.uncg.edu.

"Historic Architecture Survey Update, Phase 1-B," files.nc.gov, August 2008.

"Historic Magnolia House History," thehistoricmagnoliahouse.org.

"History," stameys.com.

"The History of Drive-In Movie Theaters (and Where They Are Now)," nyfa.edu, June 7, 2017.

Hockeydb.com.

Holmes, Erik. "Glory Days," Triad Business Journal, bizjournals.com, Aug. 15, 2005.

"Houston Franchise Sold For $650,000," Statesville Record & Landmark, p. 9, Jan. 3, 1969.

"Houston Mavericks," remembertheaba.com.

"Howard Johnson's," losttables.com.

Ingram, Billy. "Friendly Times," O. Henry Magazine, ohenrymag.com, May 2019.

Ingram, Billy. "Your New Cadillac Has Arrived," O. Henry Magazine, ohenrymag.com, February 17, 2022.

"Ivory Stores To Hold Formal Opening Of Unit Here Sat." Burlington Daily News-Times, p. 12, June 29, 1934.

Jarboe, Michelle. "Family hot dog, ice cream business nears 100," Durham Herald-Sun, p. D5, Dec. 29, 2005.

"The Jefferson Standard Building: Lower Manhattan Comes to Greensboro," preservationgreensboro.org.

"J. W. Scott Building, 113-115 West Washington Street," pocketsights.com.

"Krogering in Greensboro," groceteria.com, Dec. 1, 2018.

Levy, Shawn. "De Niro: A Life," Crown Publishing Group, United States, 2015.

"Libby Hill Seafood Restaurants," libbyhill.com.

"Lindley Family Papers, 1928-1932," archives.greensborohistory.org.

"Lindley Field," ncmarkers.com.

"Lindley Park Reopens This Coming Week," Greensboro Daily News, p. 8, April 7, 1906.

"List of dead in tornado-ravaged Greensboro swells to 12; work of relief and rehabilitation
        speeded," Burlington Daily Times-News, gendisasters.com, April 3, 1936.

"Local News," Greensboro Patriot, p. 1, Oct. 15, 1902.

Luker, Ralph E., and Richardson, Christopher M. "Historical Dictionary of the
        Civil Rights Movement," Rowman & Littlefield. United Kingdom, 2014.

"M'Lean gives flier welcome to N. Carolina," Charlotte News, p. 1, Oct. 14, 1927.

Maple, Laura. "J. Douglas Galyon Depot," theclio.com, July 9, 2015.

Martin, Jonathan. "WBTV," northcarolinahistory.org.

"Masonic Temple, 426 West Market Street," pocketsights.com.

McDowell, Ian. "Robert DeNiro debunks a local legend," yesweekly.com, Dec. 18, 2018.

McDowell, Ian. "Triad Green Book sites once sheltered black travelers," yesweekly.com,
        May 29, 2019.

McGrath, Eileen. "Carnegie Libraries," ncpedia.org, 2006.

Mills, Forest. "Southeastern Building," theclio.com, Dec. 11, 2019.

"Mitchell's Clothing owner looks back on outfitting Greensboro through the decades,"
        youtube.com, Jan. 2, 2018.

"Mitchell's Clothing Store Greensboro, NC," myhome.unctv.org.

Morgan, Thomas S. "McAlister, Alexander Worth," ncpedia.org.

"Moses Herman Cone," immigrantentrepreneurship.org.

Myers, Bob. "Moe And Jack, Naturally, Are Stars In Checkers Win," Charlotte News, p. 6,
        Jan. 14, 1963.

"National Register of Historic Places Registration Form: World War Memorial Stadium,"
        files.nc.gov, October, 1990.

"New Greensboro Bank Opens on April First," Greensboro Patriot, p. 6, Jan. 8, 1920.

"New Parking Deck Open," greensboro.com, July 30, 1990.

NFL.com.

"North Carolina May Get ABA Club," Charlotte Observer, p. D1, Jan. 5, 1969.

"North Carolina-NC 1st McDonald's," coach4aday.wordpress.com, Aug. 26, 2016.

"O. Henry Contract Let," Greensboro Patriot, p. 8, May 31, 1917.

"O. Henry Hotel Bought by Dinkler Company," Charlotte Observer, p. 19, June 7, 1936.

O. Henry Hotel mentioned in Charlotte Observer, p. 4, Dec. 30, 1916.

"O. Henry Hotel," ohenryhotel.com.

"Old Carolina Cadillac Dealership a Step Closer to National Register,"
preservationgreensboro.org.

"Old Guilford County Courthouse Celebrates a Century of Service," preservationgreensboro.org.

"Original Home Place Of The Greensboro Red Wings," waymarking.com.

"Our History," wrangler.com.

"Pancake Masters," ourstate.com, July 2011.

"Passings: Max Feldberg; Co-Founder of Zayre department stores," April 29, 1988, latimes.com.

"Preservation Greensboro Recognizes Community Revitalization in 2019," preservationgreensboro.org.

Preyer, Norris W. "Vick Chemical Company," ncpedia.org, 2006.

"The Progressive Grocer," Trade Division, Butterick Company, United States, 1930.

Puterbaugh, Parke. "The Blind Tiger sets events to celebrate its 30th anniversary," greensboro.com, July 21, 2018.

Rappoport, Ken. "UCLA Falls To Wolfpack In Double OT," Lumberton Robesonian, p. 1B, March 24, 1974.

"RIP Radio Shack," ccmallcity.blogspot.com, Feb. 9, 2015.

"S&W Cafeteria," charlotteeats.blogspot.com, Feb. 24, 2008.

"S&W Cafeteria (Greensboro, N.C.)," d.lib.ncsu.edu.

Salsi, Lynn. "Greensboro Then & Now," Arcadia Publishing, Charleston, S.C., 2007.

Schlosser, Jim. "End of an Era: Montgomery Ward to Leave Greensboro Again, This Time for Good, but the 'W' Atop the Downtown Building Will Be a Reminder the Company Was Here," greensboro.com, Jan. 27, 2001.

Schlosser, Jim. "Painting Celebrates 1950s Car Culture," greensboro.com, April 21, 2002.

Schwartz, Allan B. "Medical Mystery: In TV debate, Nixon looked nervous," inquirer.com, Sept. 24, 2016.

Scott Seed & Grocery Company ad, Greensboro Daily News, p. 11, Dec. 7, 1917.

"The Secrets of Lindley Park," preservationgreensboro.org.

Sedgefield Country Club ad, Charlotte Observer, p. B7, Sept. 3, 1925.

"S. H. Kress Building, 212 South Elm Street," pocketsights.com.

Sharpe, Martha L. S&W Cafeteria letter, greensboro.com, Sept. 28, 2018.

"Sifford Tailors Game To Greensboro Fitting," Toledo Blade, p. 25, April 14, 1961.

Sinclair, Adriana. "International Relations Theory and International Law: A Critical Approach," Cambridge University Press, 2010.

"Snead's 271 New Low for Major Tourney," Richmond News Leader, p. 14, March 29, 1938.

Snider, William D. "Greensboro News and Record," ncpedia.org, 2006.

"Son-In-Law Of Dr. Taylor Honored," Wilkesboro Journal-Patriot, p. 1, March 9, 1933.

"Souchak Victor At Greensboro By 7 Strokes," Toledo Blade, p. 21, April 17, 1961.

Statscrew.com.

"Successful Suburban Lot Sale," Greensboro Patriot, p. 1, June 1, 1904.

Tarleton, Larry. "North Carolina May Get ABA Club," Charlotte Observer, p. D1, Jan. 5, 1969.

"Tex & Shirley's Family Restaurant > Breakfast Menu," yelp.com.

"Thalhimer's," thedepartmentstoremuseum.org.

"The TJX Companies, Inc. History," fundinguniverse.com.

"Timeline of UNGC History, 1940-1949," library.uncg.edu.

"To Have a Country Club," Charlotte Observer, p. 1, Jan. 1, 1911.

Tomlin, Jimmy. "The Story of Vicks VapoRub," ourstate.com, December 2020.

"Tracing an Architecturally Brazen Greensboro, 1944-1975," preservationgreensboro.org.

"U. S. Post Office and Courthouse, 324 West Market Street," pocketsights.com.

"Victim May Have Started Theatre Fire," Durham Herald-Sun, p. 13, July 4, 1981.

Vincent, Steve. "Why is Greensboro Called 'The Gate City'?" blog.greatnest.com, Sept. 30, 2013.

"War Memorial Stadium," ncat.edu.

"WBIG Radio Collection," archives.greensborohistory.org.

Wilson, Carl. "After 45 years, Tex and Shirley's restaurant is calling it quits at Friendly," greensboro.com, Dec 24. 2017.

"Witness Sees Explosion," Burlington Daily Times News, April 14, 1973.

"Woolworth Co.," britannica.com.

"Yellowbrick Road Tour," concertarchives.org.

Also by the author

Historical nonfiction

Yesterday's Highways

America's First Highways

Highways of the South

The Great American Shopping Experience

Martinsville Memories

Fresno Growing Up

Highway 99: The History of California's Main Street

Highway 101: The History of El Camino Real

The Legend of Molly Bolin

A Whole Different League

Fiction

The Talismans of Time

Pathfinder of Destiny

Nightmare's Eve

Death's Doorstep

Memortality

Paralucidity

The Only Dragon

Identity Break

Feathercap

Praise for other works

"If you have any interest in highways, old diners and motels and such, or 20th century US history, this book is for you. It is without a doubt one of the best highway books ever published."

— Dan R. Young, founder OLD HIGHWAY 101 group, on **Yesterday's Highways**

"Profusely illustrated throughout, **Highway 99** is unreservedly recommended as an essential and core addition to every community and academic library's California History collections."

— California Bookwatch

"... an engaging narrative that pulls the reader into the story and onto the road. ... I highly recommend **Highway 99: The History of California's Main Street**, whether you're a roadside archaeology nut or just someone who enjoys a ripping story peppered with vintage photographs."

— Barbara Gossett,
Society for Commercial Archaeology Journal

"The genres in this volume span horror, fantasy, and science-fiction, and each is handled deftly. ... **Nightmare's Eve** should be on your reading list. The stories are at the intersection of nightmare and lucid dreaming, up ahead a signpost ... next stop, your reading pile. Keep the nightlight on."

— R.B. Payne, Cemetery Dance

"As informed and informative as it is entertaining and absorbing, **Fresno Growing Up** is very highly recommended for personal, community, and academic library 20th Century American History collections."

— John Burroughs, Reviewer's Bookwatch

"An essential primer for anyone seeking an entrée into the genre. Provost serves up a smorgasbord of highlights gleaned from his personal memories of and research into the various nooks and crannies of what 'used-to-be' in professional team sports."

— Tim Hanlon, Good Seats Still Available,
on **A Whole Different League**

"The complex idea of mixing morality and mortality is a fresh twist on the human condition. ... **Memortality** is one of those books that will incite more questions than it answers. And for fandom, that's a good thing."

— Ricky L. Brown, Amazing Stories

"Punchy and fast paced, **Memortality** reads like a graphic novel. ... (Provost's) style makes the trippy landscapes and mind-bending plot points more believable and adds a thrilling edge to this vivid crossover fantasy."

— Foreword Reviews

"**Memortality** by Stephen Provost is a highly original, thrilling novel unlike anything else out there."

— David McAfee, bestselling author of

33 A.D., 61 A.D., and 79 A.D.

"Provost sticks mostly to the classics: vampires, ghosts, aliens, and even dragons. But trekking familiar terrain allows the author to subvert readers' expectations. ... Provost's poetry skillfully displays the same somber themes as the stories. ... Worthy tales that prove external forces are no more terrifying than what's inside people's heads."

— Kirkus Reviews on **Nightmare's Eve**

About the author

Stephen H. Provost is the author of several books on 20th century America, covering topics that range from his hometown to department stores and shopping centers; from pop music and sports icons to the history of our nation's highways. During a 30-year career in journalism, he worked as a managing editor, sports editor, copy desk chief, columnist and reporter at five newspapers. As a novelist, he has written about dragons, mutant superheroes, and things that go bump in the night. A California native, he now lives in Virginia.

Did you enjoy this book?

Recommend it to a friend. And please consider rating it and/or leaving a brief review online at Amazon, Barnes & Noble and Goodreads.

www.ingramcontent.com/pod-product-compliance
Lightning Source LLC
Chambersburg PA
CBHW072047090426
42733CB00033B/2414